THE

wRECkiNG

YARD

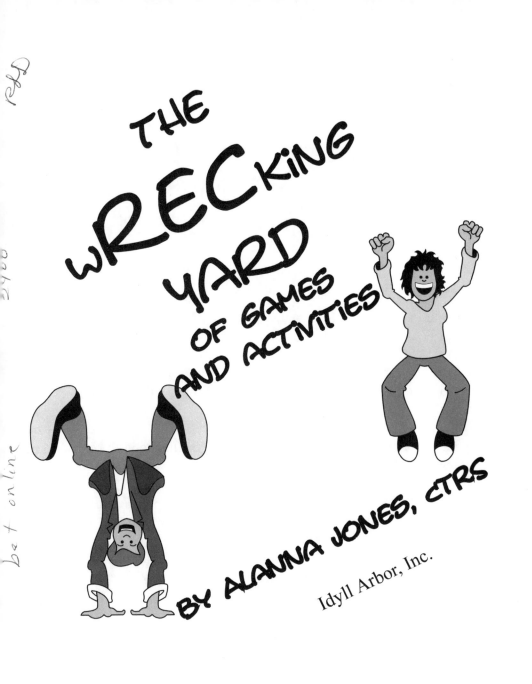

THE wRECkiNG YARD
OF GAMES AND ACTIVITIES

BY ALANNA JONES, CTRS

Idyll Arbor, Inc.

Idyll Arbor, Inc.

PO Box 720, Ravensdale, WA 98051 (425) 432-3231

372.13
Jone

Third printing, 2002

ISBN 1-882883-35-7

Dedicated to my loving husband Eric,
who never stops believing in me.

ACKNOWLEDGMENTS

A special thanks to my husband Eric for giving me encouragement and support throughout the time I was writing this book.

To my parents who helped me smooth out the rough edges.

To those who have given me some great game ideas along the way, especially Nicole Leary and Leslie Goin.

I would also like to thank the LORD above for giving me the wonderful gift of creativity which made it possible for me to write this book.

CONTENTS

Communication Skills 161

Anger Management... 191

Fitness 217

Alphabetical List of Games

INTRODUCTION

Imagine learning everything you need to know by playing games. If this were the case, I would have received all A's when I was in school. Unfortunately this wasn't the case and I had to spend a lot of time sitting in a classroom, learning a lot of things that I didn't remember later.

I wasn't able to learn all the things I needed to know by playing games but I've been lucky enough to teach youth some of the things they need to know through many different games and activities. That is the focus of this book: a book of games and activities that are intended to open the eyes of youth to the ways they can grow emotionally and physically into stronger, more healthy individuals. (Luckily, because grownups also enjoy learning and growing through games and activities, many of the ideas in this book will help adults as well.)

Programs for "at risk" youth, the classroom, youth groups, a juvenile detention center or a psychiatric hospital — these are all examples of places where teachers, therapists and counselors now work to help youth deal with their world better. In all of these settings, the games and activities in this book can be used at several different levels:

First of all, they are fun. A group of preteen or teenage youths will find many of these activities enjoyable and interesting.

Second, they each teach a lesson. By doing these activities the participants will learn something about themselves, the other members of the group or their world.

Third, they promote change. If you, as a group leader, are concerned about some of the skills and behaviors of members of the group, these activities provide a way for you to assess the current level of skill and to teach new skills and behaviors to the participants.

Regardless of the setting, there are more and more young people with problems and difficulties which show up in troubled behaviors or intense feelings and accounts of their troubled past. Using games in any of these settings as a way of addressing unacceptable behaviors and intense emotions can lead to many positive results for you and for those involved. Games can make it easier for you to lead a discussion and they open many doors for the participants, causing them to be more invested and involved in their own development. A new dimension is added to any adolescent's or child's life when games are used as a tool to address behaviors and feelings. This can be especially true in treatment settings.

When you are working with a group of children or adolescents, there are times when you should sit around in a group and talk, times when you should play games and times when mixing the two produces many positive outcomes that would not come so easily otherwise. Teaching through games gives you a chance to become more involved with the group, a chance to be more at their level and a chance to build rapport that may be difficult to build otherwise. Observing the behaviors of the people in the group is easier when the people are involved in a group game.

In a treatment or counseling setting, participants often know what is expected and can *say* what they will do next time they are angry, depressed, etc. When they play a game, they have to *act* that way. The game is real. It shows what the participant really does. If there is a problem, you can address the behaviors as they occur. You don't have to talk about a past that is gone or a speculative future.

Some people, myself included, learn best by being involved in interactive learning. Using games as a method of teaching also addresses a variety of different learning styles.

When games are used as a lead-in to a discussion, new doors are opened for people to engage in open discussion and share their feelings. The activity is a focus for the discussion. This encourages group members who usually don't discuss their thoughts and feelings to be more open. There are many benefits to using games as a tool for teaching. When games and activities become a means of learning, there are often many wonderful and unpredictable results.

ASSESSiNG THE GROUP

The first step in leading an activity is to know the needs and limitations of the group members. Many times when I am preparing a teamwork activity for a group of adolescents or children, I realize that I must be sensitive and selective when choosing a game. Some group members may have difficulty being close to other people due to sexual or other abuse. Activities like THREE-LEGGED BASKETBALL, where people are literally tied together, are simply not appropriate in these cases. Some activities require the participants to know each other fairly well and shouldn't be used with a group that is just getting together. Check the **Who** section of the activity for information about who should and shouldn't be in the group.

Most therapist have an established method of assessing people, through a series of questionnaires and/or observations. There are many assessment tools available for different populations. Whether you use a formal assessment or not, you must find a way to understand each individual in the group so that you can select your activities carefully and address as many of the different needs of the individual group members as possible, while at the same time considering each person's unique limitations and abilities.

Age is another factor that must be considered when assessing a group. It is difficult to place a specific age on each of the activities in this book due to the different levels of functioning and maturity found in youth. Use your best judgment to determine which games best fit your group. Some activities may need a minor adjustment. The assessment process makes sure that the needs of the group are being met by the games you choose.

SELECTiNG THE GAME

Once the group is assessed, it will be easy to determine which games will address the needs of the group. In school and youth group settings, the focus is on having fun and learning about yourself and the world. Teamwork games are always appropriate and are probably the most fun, but you may have concerns that need to be addressed. If you have a lot of name calling, try THE GOOD, THE BAD AND THE UGLY

BASKETBALL. If the group is just getting to know each other, try HOW I SEE YOU, HOW YOU SEE ME. There are many other good activities in the book and one of them will probably address your concerns.

When I was working in an acute care setting in a psychiatric hospital, I found that the needs of the group were constantly changing due to the number of admissions and discharges. The dynamics of the group often changed weekly and sometimes even daily. At times a majority of the group members primarily had issues regarding lack of anger control and many also lacked impulse control, as well. When this was the case, I selected a variety of games for the group that focused predominately on anger control, teamwork and communication skills in order to address the anger, how to get along with others and how to communicate feelings. Other times the group would be dealing mainly with depression. With this type of group I would focus on self-esteem, self-discovery, fitness and leisure education. There is an obvious need in a group like this for improved self-esteem, the need to talk about feelings and to learn appropriate ways to deal with depression when it occurs.

No matter what the primary issue is for any given group, it is a good idea to touch on many different topics in order to meet the diverse needs of the members of the group. Someone who is primarily depressed may have an anger control issue whereas another individual who has a history of being angry and aggressive may very well have low self-esteem.

Selecting games to address specific behaviors is important when using games as a part of therapy, but always be willing to change the focus based on the direction the game takes. Games are often unpredictable and can lead to some very unexpected, but exciting results. The main focus of one particular group that I was leading was expression of feelings. The group was made up of four boys who had been abused and neglected throughout their lives and none of them talked much about any feelings that they had. I chose to do a music activity (MUSIC MEDLEY) hoping that the boys would be able to express some of their feelings while painting pictures of how they felt when listening to different types of music.

When everyone had finished painting their pictures, each person shared with the group what they had created and had the opportunity to talk about any feelings that they had while listening to the music. One of the boys had drawn some very violent pictures of himself shooting others and of people he knew with their heads cut off. What had started out as a group focused on getting the boys to share their feelings turned into a group on how to appropriately express anger and how to deal with the intense feelings that go along with being extremely angry. Addressing issues as they arise is a part of any therapeutic activity and, if you limit yourself to a preplanned discussion, you will miss important opportunities. Choosing a game that meets the needs of the group members is important and valuable, but letting an activity take its own course often allows for an unexpected and worthwhile outcome.

LEADING THE GAME

Once you know the needs of the group and select a game, the next step is to present the game to the group. Before actually starting the activity, it is often a good idea to go over the expectations that you have for the activity so that the participants know what is expected of them when they are engaged in the activity. The top paragraph or two of each activity can be adapted as an introduction for the group.

Stating the goal or objective of the game is helpful in some situations. When I lead a group on teamwork, I say, "Today we are going to work on teamwork and I want everyone to be thinking about what you are doing to help your teammates and how you are showing good teamwork."

Sometimes you can ask the group a question before starting an activity to help them understand what you would like them to gain from the activity. In this case I may say, "Today we are going to do a self-esteem activity. What does it mean when I say 'self-esteem'?" In either case, the question or statement tells the group members what to focus on during the game.

When you introduce the game, remember to be enthusiastic. If you picked a game and you're not enthusiastic about it, how can you expect anyone else to be? If you don't expect the game to be exciting, or at least interesting, don't use it. Pick one of the other ones. You'll have a much better chance of success.

Once the game starts, let it flow naturally as much as possible. When the group is engaged in a challenging task and is struggling to figure out how to accomplish the task, the answer may be obvious to you on the sidelines. But, no matter how much you want to give them a hint or tip, don't do it unless it is absolutely necessary. When a group succeeds on its own, it gets a much greater sense of accomplishment and pride because it completed the challenging task.

During any game there may be times when you have to stop the activity or intervene and have a group discussion because of unacceptable behavior, frustration or lack of participation. I have found that mid-game discussions are often the best for getting people to recognize their own behavior. You are talking about something right as it occurs rather than waiting until later. Whenever you stop a game, ask people to identify their own behavior and to think of a way that they can improve their behavior. Whenever possible, continue with the game to give people the opportunity to improve their own behavior.

When you lead any game, the most important thing to remember is to be flexible! You may have a game planned that doesn't take as much time as you thought it would, the number of participants may suddenly change, the weather may not cooperate. Whatever happens, always have a backup plan and do your best to adapt to the situation. Don't be afraid to give some control to the group and allow them to decide if they would like to move on to a different activity. Let them make decisions regarding the group session. Often giving the group a choice increases the involvement of people in the group.

It is important to allow time at the end of the activity for discussion so that once the game has been played or the activity completed, those who participated have a chance to share their feelings about what happened during the group.

LEADING THE DISCUSSION

The discussion prompts located at the end of the activities are meant to be a guide. Remember it is always important to be flexible and let the group go in the direction that best meets the needs of those involved. When it is time for the discussion, it is best to gather the group together in a close circle, sitting on the floor or on chairs. Before asking any of the discussion questions, ask the group if they have any general observations about the activity. Sometimes this can lead to a discussion, but sometimes it is necessary to ask specific questions in order to get the discussion going.

I have seen some leaders make the mistake of being uncomfortable with silence and talking more than the participants. The more the leader talks and the more s/he points out, the less opportunity there is for people to recognize their own behavior and understand how they acted and reacted in the game or activity. The main goal for the discussion is for group members to do most of the talking and for those involved to be the ones to give feedback to their own peers. Insight into someone's behavior often has a greater effect when coming from a peer instead of a leader.

However, it is always appropriate for the leader to give feedback and observations to specific people if s/he saw something that nobody else in the group saw. In order to get everyone involved in the discussion, give specific questions to those who are quiet or who have not had the opportunity to talk due to others, who are more outspoken, monopolizing the conversation.

No matter what direction the discussion takes, it is important to end on a positive note. At times the group may be very confrontational about someone's behavior or an individual may be down on him/herself due to feeling unsuccessful when involved in the game. In cases like these, end the discussion with a positive question, such as "Name something positive that you did during group today.", "Name something that you learned in group today." or "State a goal that you can work on for the next activity." The discussion wraps up what happened in the group, helps people to focus on their own behaviors and helps to change a simple game into an awesome learning experience.

Recreation can be a valuable tool and a great asset in the learning process. It is rewarding to see the sparkle in someone's eyes when they make an impressive self-discovery. It is exciting to see a drastic improvement in someone's behavior and feelings of self-worth because of the work you have done with them. Sometimes these rewarding times are few and far between, and it is easy to get frustrated when results do not come easily. Very often we do not realize the impact that we have on people and we may never know that a simple comment or word of praise really had an effect on someone. Remember, too, that no matter how difficult a person is, you can find something good to say about what they have done before pointing out what they need to work on.

When I was a ski instructor, I would explain the technique, ski down the hill as an example and then stand at the bottom of the slope and watch each student come down the hill, giving them pointers as they reached the bottom. I was taught to always pick out something that they did well and point this out to them before telling them what they needed to do in order to improve their skiing. Sometimes finding something to praise was difficult and the best I could do was to tell them that they were holding their ski poles correctly. I always remember to think of the ski poles and, even though our work is about teaching people how to change for the better, it is also about recognizing their individual accomplishments and successes. I hope that you find this book useful and are able to utilize it in whatever setting you are working.

TEAMWORK

Teamwork can be a hard concept to get across or it can be very simple. It depends on what the people in your group have learned in their life so far. Regardless of what the members of your group know now, these activities will help them understand the many facets of teamwork better. The activities will help you teach a variety of concepts: working with others, making contributions to a team, accepting and using suggestion from all the members of the team, leading and following at appropriate times, trusting the other members of the team and working with people who have very different skill levels.

Working with others is the essence of being on a team. It is normal, and probably desirable, for members of teams to have different skill levels. As a recreational therapist in a psychiatric hospital, I often hear requests from kids to not be on a team with someone else because they "can't work together," or I hear moans of frustration when I make up the teams or put people into pairs for an activity. You will hear this kind of complaint, too, regardless of the setting you are in. When this happens (which is quite often for me, because I purposefully make up teams and pairs of people who have difficulties getting along with one another), I simply point out the awesome opportunity that they have — the opportunity to learn how to work together with someone they clash with.

If they are successful, then they are one step closer to learning how to get along with people in their lives that they have difficulties in getting along with. Once the members of your group accept this concept, they are much more willing to try to work with someone that they generally do not get along with. When the outcome is success (which it often is), they have learned more about themselves and have a new sense of pride as a result of accomplishing the challenge before them.

Challenging teamwork activities are my favorite activities to lead and often they end up being the favorite of the group as well. When people work together with others in order to accomplish a difficult task, many special things may occur among the group members. Group trust is formed, doors are opened for meaningful discussions, self-esteem is boosted when success is praised and people learn more about improving their social and communication skills.

When you are leading a group challenge activity, the discussion afterwards is often as important as the activity itself. If the group is successful, then focus the discussion on why it worked and on what each individual in the group contributed in order to make the outcome a success. If the group gives up or frustration and conflict inhibit the completion of the activity, focus the discussion on what could have been done differently. Then let them try the activity again, if time allows. In either case there is always the opportunity for people to recognize how their behavior in a teamwork activity may be similar to the behavior that they display at home or in school. Emphasizing the importance of being able to get along with others is easily done when discussing a group activity (i.e. getting along with family, co-workers, peers, on a sports team, when in a relationship, etc.).

Teamwork activities work everywhere. Therapeutic settings, church youth groups, school groups, co-workers, families and many other types of groups have found that building bonds through challenging activities is a part of making their groups work successfully.

TEAMWORK ACTIVITIES

MEGA MINI GOLF

Playing golf is an individual sport, but creating a golf course takes many different people working together to reach a common goal. In this activity each person can contribute unique ideas and listen to the ideas of others in order to make a great golf course.

Being part of a team is one of the skills that makes life easier and more fun. It can be frustrating, but it can also be exciting. There are lots more ideas and lots more people to help the ideas become real. Even the frustration of having to get people to agree isn't always so bad.

Objective

For group members to be able to work with others in a group situation, by participating in group decision making.

Who

People who need to work on being a member of a team and getting along with teammates.

Group Size

4 to 16 participants

Materials

- ➲ Large plastic cups
- ➲ Hockey sticks
- ➲ Whiffle balls or tennis balls
- ➲ Any equipment that can be used to create mini golf obstacles (i.e. cones, basketballs, jump ropes, chairs, blocks, beanbags, tables, milk cartons, boxes, tumbling mats, etc.)

Description

Use a large field or open room. Place all the equipment (except for the hockey sticks and balls) in a pile in the middle. Break the group into smaller groups of two to four members.

Each group may use a few items from the pile to create an original mini golf hole. Each group gets one of the large plastic cups to use for the hole itself. Use the cup by tipping it onto its side so that the open end is the target at the end of the mini golf hole.

Using the selected items, the group creates an obstacle in front of the cup, with a designated starting point for the ball. Once each group has completed their mini golf hole, tour the golf course as a group, allowing each group to give an explanation of their hole to the rest of the group.

Once the tour is completed, give each person a hockey stick and ball. Have the group play a round of mini golf with each small group starting the game at a different hole.

Discussion Topics

1. Did everyone in your group contribute to the creation of the golf hole? If not, why not? If so, what contribution did you make?
2. Would it have been easier or more difficult to create a mini golf hole by yourself? Why?
3. Was there any confusion about the explanation of the course once play started?

Variations

- ➲ Depending on the size of the group and the amount of time allowed, each group may be allowed to create more than one golf hole.
- ➲ With younger children it is a good idea to supply each group with a small pile of items that they must use when creating their golf hole. Also use hula hoops for the hole.
- ➲ If possible, you may use real golf clubs and golf balls.

GROUP BANNER

Creativity can be an individual process, but it can also be a group process. Sometimes it may seem easier to do a project by yourself than it is to do it with a group, but doing something with a group adds a lot more ideas and abilities.

For this activity the group, working together, creates a banner. Notice how each person's contribution adds something to the final product and how it is different than it would have been if each person had made a banner all alone.

Objective

For people to show the ability to include others in a group project. To encourage the use of teamwork to complete a project.

Who

People who need to learn how to work with others.
People who need to listen and accept other's ideas.

Group Size

2 or more

Materials

- A large piece of butcher paper
- Markers
- Tempera paint and brushes
- Glue
- Construction paper
- Any other supplies available to decorate a banner

Description

Provide the group with all of the materials needed to create a banner, to be hung somewhere in the facility. The banner may have a theme (i.e.

4th of July, Christmas, Birthday, etc.) or the group may be creative and design an original banner that represents the group.

Discussion Topics

1. Did you feel that you were included in the creation of the banner? Why or why not?
2. Do you feel that the group used teamwork? Why or why not?
3. How was sharing used, or not used, to complete this project?
4. When is it important to share?

STiCKY SPAGHETTi

Sometimes it may be easier to do a project by yourself than it is to do with others. However, sometimes it may be necessary to include others and work as a team member because we are required to do so. If this is the case (as in this activity), it is important for everyone to feel included and for no one to take over, leaving others left out.

Objective

For people to show the ability to work with others when it may be possible to work as an individual and to be able to handle frustration when it occurs.

Who

People who have difficulty working as part of a team.
People who need to learn to work with others instead of always working alone.

Group Size

3 or more

Materials

- ➲ Bag of spaghetti noodles
- ➲ Bag of marshmallows

Description

Place the marshmallows and spaghetti in a pile, on a table or on the floor, in front of the group. The task of the group is to build a tower of spaghetti and marshmallows as tall as possible. Encourage teamwork. This activity is great for observing how people are able to work with others in a group situation.

Discussion Topics

1. What was needed from the group to create the tower?
2. Did anyone become frustrated? If so, how was it handled?
3. Do you feel that the tower could have been built better? How?
4. Would anyone have preferred to work individually? Why or why not?
5. Why is it important to work with others even when it is possible to do something by yourself?

Variations

➲ Gumdrops and toothpicks may be used in place of the spaghetti and marshmallows.

CREATE A GAME

Making a decision as a group, giving and accepting ideas and getting everyone to agree on something is sometimes a difficult task. In this activity a great deal of teamwork and compromise are required. If all goes well, the end result can be fun and entertaining.

For some people in the group, coming up with original ideas and sharing them with the group will be scary unless the group is supportive and positive. Everyone needs to give ideas. They may be rejected, but they may also be praised. Acceptance and rejection are just parts of life that you need to learn how to deal with.

Each person can make the situation better for everyone else in the group, too, if they listen to everyone else and respond to them the way they want to be responded to.

Objective

For the group members to show teamwork by working together to create a new game, including all group members in the process.

Who

People who have the ability to solve problems and create new ideas, and who need to work on solving problems as a member of a group.

Group Size

2 or more

Materials

➲ Gather any equipment that you have in your facility that you think a group can use to create an original game (i.e. gym equipment for an active game or paper and pens for a board game).

Description

Designate an area (i.e. gym, outside field or room) as the place the game will take place and provide the equipment that you have gathered.

Instruct the group that they have ten minutes to work together to come up with an original game that they can play for at least ten minutes. Only the equipment provided may be used when creating the new game.

When the game has been created, have the group play the game. You may allow changes in the game as it is being played or you may have the group play without changes for some amount of time before any changes are made.

Discussion Topics

1. How did the group work together to come up with an original game?
2. What role did you take in the group and why?
3. How easy or difficult was it to make decisions as a group?
4. Can you name a time when you will need to make decisions as a member of a group? How do you anticipate you will act and why?

Variations

➲ The group may be required to use all of the items provided, rather than just some of the items.
➲ If the group is very large, split the group into smaller groups. Give each group a different set of equipment and instruct the groups to invent a new game that they will teach to the other groups.
➲ Time limits may be changed to accommodate group time.

THREE LEGGED BASKETBALL

The world is a place where we need to cooperate, at least part of the time. We can't always be on our own. Sometimes the cooperation is very close, almost like we have to step with someone else at exactly the same time. This close cooperation can be very, very difficult. Sometime we need to cooperate at a farther distance, but still working together for a team goal. This activity has some of each.

In this activity everyone is tied to a partner's leg. They better learn to move at the same time. This is really close cooperation and for some people it can be very frustrating. Everyone needs to think, though, if giving in to the frustration and getting angry is the best way to get what they want. Perhaps it is better to keep the frustration below the explosion level and learn to cooperate.

The group is also trying to play a game of basketball as a member of a team. There are all sorts of ways to play: hog the ball, give it to the stars and let them shoot, make sure everyone has a chance, teach the game to the people who are not as good and so on. During the game, everyone should try different ways of playing, just to see how they feel.

Objective

For group members to show teamwork when working together with a peer and with a group at the same time.

Who

People who need to learn to give and take. Make sure they can handle being in very close proximity to others.

Group Size

8 to 16 participants

Materials

➲ Bandannas or cloth strips
➲ Basketball
➲ Basketball hoop

Description

Divide the group into two even teams, then divide each team into pairs. Tie each pair together at the ankle, using the strips of cloth. The teams are now ready to play a game of three legged basketball.

Play the game using more or less normal basketball rules. Be prepared for frustration from being tied together and change partners as required.

Discussion Topics

1. What was difficult about this game?
2. What do you feel that you did, if anything, to help make the game easier for you and your partner? for your team?
3. How well do you feel that you do at working with others and why is it important to be able to work with others?
4. How do you think that your partner did at this activity and why?
5. Has there ever been a time when you have made an activity difficult for others? What happened and why?
6. Name a time in your life when you had to cooperate with others to make things easier, and what you did?

Variations

➲ If the group is large, play tournament style and rotate the teams.
➲ If the group is small (or low functioning) play a game of three legged "Horse" instead.

WATER CARRY CHALLENGE

Solving a problem and working together to find the answer often takes a whole team. Each person has his or her own contribution to make and is an important part of the team.

This activity takes everyone's participation and contribution. Otherwise, the group may not be able to finish the task. This one is hard enough, they might not be able to finish anyway, unless someone in the group does some very creative thinking.

Objective

For group members to recognize the importance of using teamwork in a group situation. For people to show the ability to handle frustration when it is encountered.

Who

People who have the ability to problem solve but need to work on problem solving as a member of a group. People who can handle significant frustration.

Group Size

4 to 12 participants

Materials

- ⊃ Ten paper cups filled three fourths full of water
- ⊃ Cafeteria tray

Description

Place half of the cups filled with water on the floor at one end of a room and place the remaining cups at the other end. Gather the group together in the middle of the area and give them the cafeteria tray. Instruct the group that their task is to get each container onto the tray without spilling any of the water and that they must follow the following rules:

1. Everyone in the group may stand on only one foot and is allowed to use only one hand during the entire activity.
2. Only one cup may be picked up from an end of the room at a time, you then must pick up a cup from the other end. Continue to alternate ends of the room until all the cups are on the tray.
3. The tray must be carried to the cups, the cups may not be carried to the tray.
4. The tray must be carried and not slid on the ground.
5. If any of the water spills out of the cup, all of the cups on the tray must be put back onto the floor where they started from.
6. Once all of the cups are on the tray, the tray should be placed on the floor in the middle of the room, at which point the task is completed.

(The only way that I have found to complete this activity is to pass the tray from one person to the next while they are standing still. Have the person at the end of the line hop to the front of the line to get the tray across the room.)

Discussion Topics

1. Was it necessary to use teamwork? Why or why not?
2. How was communication important during this task?
3. Was there frustration in the group at all? If so, how was it handled?
4. How did you feel when the group was required to start over? What made the group keep going?
5. Was anyone tempted to quit? Why?
6. How did it feel when the group was finally successful?
7. How can you relate this activity to your life?

DiSABiLiTY OBSTACLE COURSE

We all have obstacles in our lives that we must overcome. Some obstacles and disabilities require us to get help from others and sometimes we must help those who have a disability.

This game is a great learning experience as well as a great teamwork activity. Only when the group members realize that they must help each other and accept help from others, will they be able to succeed.

Objective

For group members to rely on each other's help to complete the task successfully. To promote awareness of living with disability.

Who

People who need to learn it is okay to accept help from others.
People who need to learn to help other.

Group Size

6 to 12 participants

Materials

- An existing obstacle course (or create one with supplies and equipment from the facility)
- Bandannas or cloth strips
- Cotton balls
- A wheelchair (if available)

Description

Assign each member of the group a different disability. Everyone pretends to have their disability while the group attempts to go through the obstacle course successfully together.

Use the cloth strips or bandannas to make the disabilities more realistic by tying someone's ankles or wrists together, an arm to a side or an ankle to a thigh with a bent leg. Someone may be given the role of a person who is not able to talk and someone else may be free of any disabilities. Use cotton balls to make someone hard of hearing, cloth strips as blindfolds and, if a wheelchair is available, use it, too. Someone may also be assigned the role of being unconscious and must act the part.

Once everyone has assumed their roles, instruct the group that they need to get everyone through the obstacle course successfully and that they must stay together as a group.

Discussion Topics

1. How dependent were you on the other members of the group?
2. Were you able to let others help you? Did you like it or not?
3. Do you have a disability in your life that requires you to depend on others for assistance? If so, how do you feel about needing help from someone else?

Variations

- If the group is large, then split the group into teams and have each team go through the course separately or start at different points in the course but go through it at the a same time.
- The same disability may be assigned to more than one person or you may give an individual more than one disability.
- If a large outdoor area is available, make a map of the area. The course may be drawn out using the natural obstacles found in the area.

COOKiE BAKE

When we cook, we use cookbooks to guide us. When there are no cookbooks, the simple task of making cookies becomes a challenge. In this activity the group must work together, without a recipe, to figure out how to make a tasty treat that everyone can enjoy in the end.

Objective

For people to show the ability to work with others and to be able to take part in group decision making.

Who

People who need to learn how to deal with uncertainty.
People who need to learn how to work with others on a project or job when there are no clear-cut rules to follow.

Group Size

3 or more

Materials

- Butter
- Flour
- Sugar
- Baking soda
- Brown sugar
- Salt
- Vanilla
- Eggs
- Chocolate chips
- Cookie sheets
- Oven for baking

Description

Supply the group with the ingredients to make chocolate chip cookies, as well as cookie sheets, but no other cooking utensils. Do not give the group the recipe and instruct the group that their task is to make edible cookies with the ingredients given, then let them go to it.

You may supply approximately the correct amount of each ingredient or you may not, depending on the group.

Discussion Topics

While cookies are baking:
1. Do you feel the cookies will turn out good or bad? Why?
2. How did the group work together to make the cookies?
3. What part did you have in making the cookies?

After the cookies are baked:
1. How did the cookies turn out?
2. How would you do things differently another time?
3. Who turned out to be the best cook? How did the group use that person's information?

BLIND OBSTACLE COURSE

When you are responsible for someone else, remember that the other person is trusting you to do your job and keep him/her safe. When you are relying on other people, being able to trust them is important.

This game requires trust as well as teamwork. Building trust among group members is an important aspect of building relationships. Once trust is formed, people begin to feel more comfortable sharing feelings with one another. This game may be just the thing to start the process of building trust and relationships among the group.

Objective

For group members to recognize the importance of using clear verbal communication skills when working with others. To practice and understand the importance of having good listening skills. To establish trust among group members.

Who

People who need to learn to trust others.
People who need to learn to give trustworthy advice.
People who need to work on communication and direction skills and share responsibility with others.

Group Size

2 or more

Materials

- ⊃ Blindfolds
- ⊃ An existing obstacle course or equipment for creating an obstacle course

Description

Divide the group into pairs and blindfold one member of each pair. The person without the blindfold guides the person with the blindfold through the obstacle course. Do not let the people who are blindfolded see the obstacle course prior to being blindfolded.

The blindfolded people may only be guided through the course by listening to the verbal directions given to them by their respective partner. No touching is allowed.

After the first person goes through the course, switch the blindfold to the other person. Repeat the process with the same obstacle course or with a different course.

Discussion Topics

1. Was it easier to give directions or to receive directions? Why?
2. How was trust involved in this activity?
3. Do you find it easier to talk or to listen? Why?
4. Was it easier for the first person or the second person? Why?
5. Would it be easier if you could touch the person instead of having to lead by talking?
6. In your life, when is it important for you to have good communication skills?

Variations

➲ Prior to putting a blindfold on anyone, have half of the group work together to create an obstacle course with the equipment provide and, at the same time, the other half of the group creates a different course somewhere else. Once both the courses are completed, pair the groups up so that one person from each group is paired up with one person from the other group and they each lead their partners through the course that their group created. This is a great way to combine group teamwork with a communication and trust activity.

ROOT BEER FLOAT LiFEBOAT

Trying to get your needs met is often hard. It's even harder when everyone else is trying to get their needs met, too, and what they do can make it easier or harder for you.

In this activity everyone's fate is linked together, literally, as you try to make a root beer float for yourself and everybody else. Being able to work as a group so that everyone gets what they want will lead to some very tasty results. (Not cooperating could end up with all the good stuff on the floor.)

Objective

For group members to use teamwork to accomplish a task. For people to demonstrate appropriate social skills by demonstrating the ability to think of the needs of others in the group.

Who

People who need to understand how the needs of everyone in a group are interconnected. Make sure everyone can handle being tied together.

Group Size

2 or more

Materials

- ⊃ Bandannas or cloth strips
- ⊃ Root beer
- ⊃ Vanilla ice cream
- ⊃ Cups
- ⊃ Spoons
- ⊃ Ice cream scoop

Description

Place all of the ingredients to make a root beer float on a table, with the group gathered around the table. Use the bandannas or cloth strips to tie the wrist of each member in the group to the wrist of his/her neighbors on each side. The group should form a circle around the table.

If everyone in the group wants a root beer float, the group must figure out a way to work together to accomplish this task. This is a fun activity, with a great reward for being successful when the task is accomplished.

Discussion Topics

1. What was required from the group for everyone to get a root beer float?
2. Did the root beer float motivate you to work harder to accomplish the task? What if water and cups were all you had been given?
3. Was there any frustration from any of the group members at any time? If so how was it handled?
4. Do you feel that the people on both sides of you considered your needs or were they just concerned with getting their own needs met? How did this make you feel?

Variations

➲ Other foods, or a task, may be substituted for the root beer float (i.e. wrapping a package or peanut butter and jelly sandwiches for lunch)
➲ May be done in pairs instead of in a group.

BLIND EARTHBALL SOCCER

Giving and receiving clear instructions is an important part of teamwork for any group that is working together to compete a task. In this game the team that works together the best is the team that will win in the end.

The group members need to listen to their teammates when they are pushing the ball and think carefully about the information they give when they are watching. Being able to trust the other people on the team is vital for success.

Objective

For group members to achieve an end goal through teamwork. To establish trust among group members.

Who

People who need to learn how to trust others, be trusted, communicate and listen to others.

Group Size

4 or more

Materials

➲ Blindfolds
➲ Earthball (or large, soft ball)

Description

Divide the group into two teams. Line one team up on one side of the play area and one team on the other side, facing each other. Place the earthball in the middle of the play area.

Blindfold one member of each team and face both of them toward the earthball, standing on their team lines. The teams then wait for the signal from the leader to "go." Once the signal is given, the blindfolded individuals, without using their hands, attempt to get to the earthball and to get the ball to the line of the other team for a score. At the same time they try to stop the opponent from getting the ball past them to their own team's line.

Teammates that are on the line may not step over the line but may yell directions to their blindfolded teammate to guide him or her to the earthball and to keep him or her from getting hurt. Once the ball crosses one of the lines or the leader decides the match is a tie, switch the blindfolds to other members of each team until everyone has a chance to be blindfolded.

Discussion Topics

1. When blindfolded, did you rely on your teammates? If not, why not? If so, how did your teammates help you?
2. Was trust a factor in this activity? If so, how?
3. In your life is there ever a time when it helps to have guidance from others? If so, when?
4. In what ways have you guided others?

Variations

➲ If the earthball is large, allow the players to use their hands to move the ball across the line.
➲ For more skilled groups a regular soccer ball may be used.
➲ Blindfold more than one person on each team at a time.

PARTNER CARD TOWER

Being totally dependent on someone else is often difficult and frustrating. Being able to work as a team and to overcome the frustration is important.

It's hard enough to build a tower of cards in the best of circumstances. This is not the best of circumstances, as you will see. Everyone needs to work together with his/her partner if the pair hopes to accomplish anything at all.

Objective

For people to show frustration tolerance when attempting to accomplish a difficult task. For people to show the ability to use communication skills when working with a teammate, in order to accomplish a difficult task.

Who

People who need to learn how to work with others under frustrating conditions.

Group Size

2 or more

Materials

➲ One deck of playing cards for every two people in the group.

Description

Divide the group into pairs, giving each pair a deck of cards. Instruct the group that their task is to use the deck of cards to build a tower of cards as high as they can.

When building the tower, each partner may use only one hand and must place the other hand behind his/her back. Encourage teams to build as tall a tower as they possibly can and to start over each time the cards fall. It is a good idea to set a time limit for this activity and see who has the tallest tower once the time is up.

Discussion Topics

1. What was needed from you and your partner to accomplish this task?
2. Was anyone frustrated at any time during the activity? If so, how was it handled?
3. How important would your partner's help have been if you both could have used two hands?

Variations

➲ Start with both hands, halfway through switch to one hand and compare the difference.
➲ Use your best hand part of the time and your other hand part of the time and compare them.

CREATE A SKIT

Actors, actresses, writers and directors must work closely together to make a final production that people will want to see. For this activity the group must work closely together, filling all of these roles, to create a skit.

Once each group comes together and uses teamwork to create a play, there is a show to present what was created. The more good ideas from everyone, the better the show will be.

Objective

For group members to demonstrate teamwork and to promote creativity.

Who

People who have the ability to be creative but need to learn how to create something in a group setting.

Group Size

6 or more

Materials

➲ Brown paper bags
➲ Anything available to be used in a simple skit as props (i.e. paper cup, balloon, pencil, plastic spoon, deck of cards, party hat, etc.)

Description

Break up the group into teams of three to five participants each. Supply each team with a bag filled with various props to be used in a skit. Allow five to ten minutes for each team to plan an original skit using all of the props in their bag and including all of the members of their team. Each skit is then performed for the rest of the group.

Discussion Topics

1. Was this task easy or difficult for your group? Why?
2. Were you happy with the skit that your group performed? Why or why not?
3. When making decisions as a group, what is important?
4. Are you ever faced with the task of making a decision as a member of a group in your life? If so, what role do you usually take?

GROUP JUMP ROPE

Sometimes it's better to have more people involved. Sometimes it just makes things worse. This activity is much more challenging because everyone is involved. Everyone will have to work together and, even harder, jump at exactly the same time.

Setting a possible goal and working hard to reach that goal is a big part of being able to work together on a team.

Objective

For group members to work together as a team in order to successfully complete the task given to them.

Who

People who need to learn to work with others.
People who need to learn to be more tolerant of others who are more or less skilled than they are.

Group Size

5 or more

Materials

➲ An extra long jump rope or many smaller ropes tied together

Description

Ask the group to set a group goal of how many jumps they think the group can do consecutively without anyone making a mistake. This can be a difficult activity so you may want to try to lower expectations rather than get them too high, depending on the group. Four or five jumps is about the limit for most groups.

Chose two people to turn the jump rope while the rest of the group attempts to successfully jump rope all at the same time.

Take turns with the people turning the rope so that everyone gets a chance to try both parts of the activity.

Discussion Topics

1. Was the group successful at this activity? Why or why not?
2. What did it take for the group to be successful at this task?
3. What did you contribute to the group?
4. What happened when one person in the group had a difficult time with this activity?
5. When has it been important for you to contribute 100% to a group?
6. How can we help others who have difficulties when they are in a group activity with us?

Variations

- ⊃ If the group can't make even one jump, limit the number of jumpers in each group.
- ⊃ Make the challenge to see how many people can make a jump at the same time instead of seeing how many jumps the whole group can make.

PUZZLE MiX

Putting together a puzzle with more than one person doing the work may seem simple. However, teamwork and group communication are necessary to insure that everyone in the group is included and no one is left out.

Sometimes we may be so focused on completing a task that we forget to accept help from others. This activity is not about reaching a goal. It is about sharing, including everyone and communicating.

Objective

For the group to include all of its members in the activity. For people to practice appropriate social skills when working with others.

Who

People who have difficulty working as part of a team.
People who need to learn to work with others rather than alone.

Group Size

2 or more

Materials

➲ 2 or more jigsaw puzzles (100 pieces or less)
➲ Bag

Description

Empty all of the puzzle pieces into one bag and mix them up. Empty the bag out for the group with instructions to sort out all of the pieces and put together all of the puzzles. To make it more challenging do not allow the participants to see the pictures on the front of the puzzle boxes.

Discussion Topics

1. Do you feel that everyone had an equal part in putting the puzzles together?
2. Did you feel included or excluded in this activity? Why?
3. How did you make sure you got to help or how did you make sure others were included in this activity?
4. When in your life has it been important for you to include others and/or yourself in an activity? What did you do and why?

RLiND SQUARE OBSERVATiON

Everyone can't be the leader when a group is working together. Of course, everyone can't follow either. There must be a balance.

In this activity you need to find a balance between leaders and followers and, since nobody knows everything that is going on, each person will need to do a little of both leading and following. Everyone will need to work together to accomplish this task.

Objective

For people to learn what role they take when involved in a group project and to find out how to shift roles as required by the project.

Who

People who need to learn to give ideas, accept ideas and take on appropriate roles in a group.

Group Size

4 or more

Materials

➲ One long rope (the two ends tied together to form a circle)
➲ Blindfolds
➲ Video camera, video tape, VCR (if available)

Description

Blindfold each member of the group and place the rope on the floor in front of the group. Instruct the group that they must form a square, using the rope. If you are using a video camera, do not allow anyone to see it prior to being blindfolded.

Once the group has decided that they have made a square, allow them to take off their blindfolds and look at the shape that they created. Prior to discussion time, watch the video as a group. If you are not using a video camera, discuss the activity at this point.

Discussion Topics

1. What did the group do in an attempt to complete the task?
2. Did you help or hinder the group? How?
3. What did you observe from the video that showed how you helped or hindered the group?
4. How was teamwork a factor in this activity?

Variations

➲ Ask the group to make different shapes (i.e. form the shape of a letter or a number).

GiFT WRAP CHALLENGE

Moving in the same direction and working towards the same goal isn't always easy for a group of people to do. Even though it isn't easy, it is often very important to be able to work towards the same goal with others.

In this activity people will find that wrapping the boxes is a little harder than it would be normally, but with teamwork and communication the group can be successful and maybe even have some fun in the process.

Objective

For people to show teamwork when working with a partner to complete a project.

Who

People who need to learn to work with others and can handle close contact in a frustrating situation.

Group Size

2 or more

Materials

(For every 2 people)
- ➲ Empty cardboard box
- ➲ Wrapping paper
- ➲ Tape
- ➲ Scissors
- ➲ 2 bandannas or cloth strips
- ➲ Optional: ribbon, card, markers

Description

Divide the group into pairs. Have each pair face each other and hold out their arms towards each other. Tie each pair together with the cloth or bandannas so both wrists are tied. The right wrist of one person is tied to the left wrist of the other person.

Give them their supplies for the activity. Instruct the group that they must wrap their package as neatly as they can. Once everyone is finished, show the finished products to the rest of the group.

Discussion Topics

1. What did you and your partner have to do in order to wrap your package successfully?
2. Are you happy with the way your package looks? Why or why not?
3. Did you both work equally together or do you feel that one person did more of the work? Why did this happen?
4. Did you and your partner have any difficulties when working together? Why or why not?
5. Can you think of a time in your life when it is important for you to be able to work together with someone else?
6. What is important for you to do in order to work together with someone else successfully?

Variations

➲ Do this activity around Christmas time for actual gifts that need to be wrapped.
➲ Tie more than 2 people together to form a larger group.

OVER UNDER

Even though it isn't easy, it is often very important to be able to work with others towards the same goal. Sometimes, if just one person in the group is not working with the rest of the team, the goal cannot be reached. This game is about everyone working together to accomplish a goal, with each person doing his/her best to contribute.

Even if other people are not as skillful or are much more skillful, you still need to work with them to be successful in life. An important part of this activity is trying to figure out a pattern or order of play that will help the whole team succeed.

Objective

For all the people in the group to work together to meet a team goal.

Who

People who need to learn how to be part of a team, how to make a contribution to the team and how to work with other people who have different skill levels.

Group Size

4 or more

Materials

- ⊃ Volleyball net
- ⊃ Volleyball or beach ball

Description

The entire group starts on one side of the net with the goal of getting the entire team on the other side of the net. One person starts with the ball and hits it into the air to a teammate who then hits it to another teammate. Continue in this pattern until everyone has hit the ball. Once a person hits the ball, s/he runs under the net. Before long, the entire team should be on the other side of the net except for the last person who must hit it over the net to the rest of the team before running under the net to join everyone on the other side.

Once the ball reaches the other side, the game continues as it did on the first side until someone catches the ball or the ball hits the ground. At that point the game starts over with everyone back on the same side of the net again. Have the group set a goal for itself for how many times they can get the ball over the net without making a mistake.

Discussion Topics

1. Was the task successfully completed? Why or why not?
2. What was required from the group for this task to be completed successfully? Was this done?
3. What part did you play in this activity?
4. What is important to remember when working with a group of different people who all have different skill levels?

Variations

➲ Put half the group on one side of the net and half on the other side. Each time someone hits the ball, they must hit it over to the other side before running under the net. The goal is to end up with both teams intact and on the opposite side of the net from where they started.

TOWEL VOLLEYBALL

Working with a partner and as a member of a team creates an added challenge for each person involved in this activity. Everyone must do their part to help their partner, their team and the entire group succeed.

This game is about team members contributing and doing their best. If one person doesn't, everyone else will feel the effect. Make sure the group notices the best way to work well with partners and with the rest of the team.

Objective

For people to use cooperation and teamwork when working with a partner and a team at the same time.

Who

People who need to learn how to work with others as a member of a team and how to allow for different skill levels from people they are working closely with.

Group Size

8 to 16 participants (an even number is best)

Materials

- ➲ One towel for every 2 participants
- ➲ Volleyball net
- ➲ Volleyball

Description

Divide the group into pairs, giving each pair a towel. Divide the sets of partners into two teams, placing one team on each side of the net. Each individual holds onto one side of the towel while his/her teammate holds onto the other side. The ball is thrown and caught using only the towel during this game.

The goal for the group is to get the ball over the net successfully as many times as possible without letting the ball touch the ground. On any given play the ball must be passed around so that each set of partners catches and tosses the ball to their teammates before the ball is tossed over the net to the other team.

Discussion Topics

1. Was this task difficult or easy? Why?
2. What was required of everyone to make this game successful?
3. How was teamwork a factor in this activity?
4. Name something positive that your partner did.
5. Name something positive that your teammates did.

Variations

➲ Use one bed sheet for each side with the entire team working together to catch and throw the ball.
➲ Play with regular volleyball rules using the towels.
➲ Use water balloons instead of a ball.

GROUP HOP

Timing, talking and a little bit of coordination are all the group needs for this activity. Of course, they need to keep trying until everyone can move together at the same time.

If it doesn't come easy, there may be a tendency to give up. When we are able to overcome frustration and the urge to quit, we accomplish a lot more than we ever knew we could. And success becomes just a bit sweeter.

Objective

For each individual to contribute to an end goal in a group activity.

Who

People who need to learn how to work with others and how to keep trying even when things get difficult.

Group Size

3 or more

Materials

➲ None

Description

Line the group up in single file, one behind the other. Each person lifts up his/her right foot and the person in front of him/her grabs onto the leg, using the right hand. The person in the front of the line lifts up his/her right leg and holds it in the air.

The group then attempts to hop forward as an entire group. Have the group set a goal of how many consecutive hops it can make and attempt to reach that goal.

Discussion Topics

1. Was this activity difficult for the group? Why or why not?
2. What was required to make this successful?
3. What did you contribute to the group?

SELF-ESTEEM

Each individual has a different path that will lead to improved self-esteem. For some it is learning how to take and give compliments. For others it is finally recognizing what it means to have good self-esteem and to recognize where they get their own self-esteem from. Still others find improved self-esteem by learning new skills and recognizing the vast potential that they have inside of them. Activities can be used in many different ways to tap into this positive potential.

A simple thing, such as being more assertive, can be a key factor in raising the self-esteem of a child or teenager. Such was the case of a young girl who was in the psychiatric hospital where I worked. She was always giving in to others, feeling like she wasn't worthwhile or in control of her own life. This led to her depression and ultimately to an eating disorder. One of the main goals that she and I decided that she needed to work on was for her to become more assertive. At first she was reluctant to speak up or even take a small leadership role in the group. She received a lot of support from her peers, who continually reminded her of her goal and didn't allow her to stay in the background, as she tended to do. Eventually she was able to speak her mind and then to plan and lead an entire activity that she was actually very excited about leading. After leading the activity, she was able to accept compliments from her peers about the good job that she had done. All because of working on a simple thing, being more assertive, her self-esteem went up and she learned valuable life skills along the way.

Self-esteem is one of those important things that we need in order to succeed. If we don't think we can do something, we can't, because we don't try. There are many aspects to self-esteem. People need to know that they have some value just because they exist. We need to be able to hear good things about ourselves without automatically rejecting them. We need to understand that negative comments about us are not always true. The bottom line is that we need to accept ourselves, know that we can change and then work to make ourselves better.

SELF-ESTEEM
ACTIVITIES

PASS IT ON

Giving compliments to others isn't always very easy to do. For some it is even harder to receive them. Good self-esteem is often the result of hearing positive things from others.

In this activity members of the group get the chance to give compliments and also get to receive them.

Objective

To increase one's self-esteem by receiving positive comments from others.

Who

People with poor self-esteem who need to learn to give and receive compliments.

Group Size

4 or more

Materials

- ➲ Paper
- ➲ Pens, pencils

Description

Supply each person with a piece of paper and a pen or pencil. Instruct everyone in the group to write his/her name on the top of the piece of paper and to then place it in the center of the group. Once all the papers are in the middle, everyone takes somebody else's paper and writes an anonymous, positive comment or note to that person before returning the sheet to the middle. Each member of the group continues to pick up different sheets from the middle until they have written a positive comment or note on everyone's paper.

Once everyone has written on all of the papers, each participant takes his/her own and takes time to read the comments silently. These make great keepsakes for people to pull out and read when they are feeling sad or down on themselves.

Discussion Topics

1. Did you find it easy to write a compliment out for everyone? Why or why not?
2. How did it feel to read the compliments?
3. Is it easier for you to give or receive compliments? Why?

INCLUDE

Feeling like you belong to a group and feeling included are often important factors in how you feel about yourself. Often people who feel a sense of belonging overlook the fact that there may be others in the group who feel left out and rejected. Recognizing the feelings that go along with feeling included or rejected are important. This activity helps group members improve their own self-esteem along with helping others feel good about themselves.

Objective

For people to understand what self-esteem is and to recognize where self-esteem comes from. To learn how to improve one's own self-esteem.

Who

People who don't feel like they belong or fit into a group.
Dominant group members who need to recognize how it feels to be left out.

Group Size

3 or more

Materials

➲ Directions and materials for any of the games in the teamwork chapter
➲ Question sheet (found on following page)
➲ Pens, pencils

Description

Choose any of the games found in the teamwork chapter. When giving the game directions, emphasize the use of teamwork to complete the task. Instead of using the discussion prompts in the teamwork activity, use the work sheet found on the following page to focus the discussion on feelings of being included or rejected and discuss how these feelings affect the self-esteem of people.

Once the group has completed the activity, hand out question sheets for each person to fill out individually. Discuss the answers to the questions on the sheet and discuss feelings in regards to the activity and worksheet.

Include Question Sheet

1. Did this activity frustrate you at all? Why or why not?

2. What role did you have in the group?

3. Was there any time when you felt excluded from the group?

4. If you felt included, what made you feel included?

5. How do you feel about yourself as a person after participating in this activity? Explain...

TEAM LEADERSHIP

Being a strong and positive leader is a good way to feel important and self-confident. Some people seem like they are born to be leaders while others have to work hard to learn the skills.

This activity gives each person in the group a chance to be the leader as s/he presents a new game to the group. This will build self-confidence and improve self-esteem in the process. The other important lesson of this activity is to teach the group members that they need to be good followers as well as good leaders for the group to be successful.

Objective

To teach leadership skills and to help people recognize the many different styles of leadership that occur within a group. To teach the group how to make decisions in a group situation and how to find new activities through the use of leisure resources. To increase self-esteem by promoting leadership skills.

Who

People who lack confidence in their leadership skills.

Group Size

4 or more

Materials

➲ As many books or resources containing game ideas as you can find
➲ Paper
➲ Pens, pencils

Description

Two sessions are required for this activity. Divide the group into smaller groups of two to four people. Supply the groups with game resource books for them to use and instruct each group to pick out a new game that they will have to teach to the rest of the group in a later session.

The games must be cleared through the leader to insure that the necessary equipment is available, that the game is appropriate for the group and that time is available for the game.

Once the games are selected and cleared through the leader, allow time for each of the groups to write down the instructions and rules to their games and to spend time planning out how the game will be led and what role each member of the group will have when leading the new activity. At a later group session or sessions, allow time for each group to introduce their new game while practicing leadership skills and, of course, having a lot of fun learning new games in the process.

Discussion Topics

1. What was difficult about working as a group in a leadership situation? What was easy?
2. What are qualities of a good leader?
3. (When group is in a circle) Name a positive leadership trait that the person on your right displayed during this activity.
4. When is it important to be able to have strong leadership qualities? What about being a good follower?

Variations

➲ Meet separately with a small group of select participants who would benefit from being put in a leadership position. Allow them to plan and lead an entire group activity to build self-esteem. Have the group focus on the positive traits of these leaders during discussion time.

GiFT FROM THE HEART

Giving and receiving gifts is often a very special and magical event. The giver expresses caring for the receiver by selecting something s/he feels would be appreciated. The receiver gets a token of affection and love.

This activity is about giving your understanding of others to them and learning how others see you through the exchange of thoughtful gifts.

Objective

To build relations among group members through positive interactions and to increase self-esteem by receiving thoughtful gifts from others.

Who

People with low self-esteem who could benefit from being thoughtful and nice toward others.

Group Size

2 or more

Materials

- ➲ Paper
- ➲ Pens, pencils
- ➲ Colored markers or crayons

Description

Each member of the group chooses an imaginary gift to give to each person in the group. Each gift is drawn or described on a piece of paper to be given to the recipient. The gifts should be thought out so they represent the individuals who receive the gifts.

The gifts may be deep and thoughtful such as "courage to face life's difficulties", for someone who has shared many deep problems with the group. Or the gifts may simply be something the receiver would enjoy, such as "a season ski pass to go skiing any time you want," for someone who enjoys skiing.

Once everyone has completed their gifts, let one person at a time give out his/her gifts to the others. When giving the gifts, the giver should explain what the gift is and why s/he chose to give that particular gift to that individual.

Discussion Topics

1. How did you decide what gifts to give?
2. What did you think about the gifts you got?
3. Do you think there was a good match between the people and the gifts they received?

Variations

➔ If group is large, assign each person a select number of group members to create a gift for, or break the large group into smaller groups.

THE GOOD, THE BAD AND THE UGLY BASKETBALL

If someone has poor self-esteem, it is often the result of hearing many negative comments throughout his/her life. For some people it is an every day thing and they don't even realize that it is happening.

Recognizing how negative comments can effect self-esteem is an important part of learning how to feel positive about yourself. As the group plays this game, the people should pay attention to how different they feel when they hear good things about themselves instead of bad things. The team members should also pay attention to whether their team does better when it is positive or negative.

Objective

To recognize how we are affected by negative and positive comments that we hear and to discuss ways to be a positive person, instead of being a negative person.

Who

People who have low self-esteem as a result of hearing negative comments throughout their lives.
People who put other people down.

Group Size

4 to 10 participants

Materials

- Basketball
- Basketball hoop

Description

Divide the group into two teams, as you would for a regular game of basketball. Inform one team that they may only say positive comments during the basketball game and the other team that they may only say negative comments. It may be necessary to set some boundaries (i.e. no swearing or racist comments) depending upon the group.

Halfway through the game, switch roles, so that the negative team is positive and the positive team is negative. This game needs to be closely monitored because at times the negative team may carry it a bit too far. In this case, cut the game short and increase the discussion time.

Discussion Topics

1. Was it fun to be negative? Why?
2. What feelings did you have during this game?
3. Were your feelings different between when your team was positive and when it was negative?
4. Do you feel that society is mostly negative or mostly positive?
5. How can you become a mostly positive person?
6. Did your team do better when the comments were positive or negative?

Variations

➲ Almost any game may be substituted for basketball, based on the size of the group and equipment available in your facility.

BUTTERFLY BEGINNINGS

Growing and changing is an important part of making your life better. Setting positive, reachable goals is a way to feel in control of making a change or growing into a better person.

Butterflies represent change from something ugly to something beautiful. Just as caterpillars can change, so can we.

Objective

To explore the things that people would like to change in order to better themselves. To encourage goal setting and the accomplishment of goals.

Who

People who have low self-esteem and want to make themselves better.

Group Size

1 or more

Materials

- Brown paper lunch bags
- Marking pens
- Colored paper
- Glue
- Pipe cleaners
- Optional: googly eyes, glitter, paint, felt

Description

Give each person a paper lunch bag to represent a butterfly cocoon. On the outside of the bag ask each person to write down his/her name and the things that s/he wishes to change about him/herself.

Once everyone has completed this activity, discuss how a cocoon represents old life and how butterflies represent new life. After the discussion, supply the group with art supplies so that each person can create a beautiful butterfly to represents new life.

When the butterflies are completed, each person places his/her butterfly in the cocoon that s/he had made earlier and seals the bag. The sealed cocoon should be placed where the group meets regularly to be reopened at a later time. Reopen the bags when people have made the changes that are stated on the outside of the bag and display the new beginning butterfly in a place for all to see.

Discussion Topics

For creating the bags:
1. How do you feel about this plan to change?
2. Do you think you will succeed? Why?

For opening the bags:
1. How do you feel about accomplishing these changes?
2. Did you think you would make it?
3. Did you ever have any doubts about yourself? How did you get over them?

Variations

➲ Write down a specific goal on the outside of the bag and open the bag once the individual reaches the goal.
➲ Put all of the butterflies in a large bag and write down group goals on the outside of the bag. Release all of the butterflies once the group reaches its goals.

TATTLE TALE

Sometimes the world we live in is a very negative place, but it really doesn't have to be. If people are used to hearing negative comments all the time, they might not even realize how many there are. It is possible to change our environment, but we have to understand it first.

This activity will help group members see what kind of world they are in right now. Perhaps it will also show them what they can do to make their world a little better.

Objective

To compare the number of positive comments made during a game to the number of negative comments made and to recognize how people are affected by these negative and positive comments.

Who

People who are in a negative environment and are not aware of it.
People who put others down.
People who have low self-esteem caused by hearing too many negative comments throughout their lives.

Group Size

6 or more

Materials

➲ Board or card games
➲ Paper
➲ Pens, pencils

Description

Separate the group into smaller groups of no more than six people per group. Supply each group with a board game or a game of cards to play. Give each person in each group a piece of paper with one of the following headings on the top. Instruct them to fold the top of the paper over so no one else in the group will know what heading is on their paper.

1. Positive statements made...
2. Negative statements made...
3. Acts of good sportsmanship...
4. Acts of poor sportsmanship...
5. Humorous statements made...
6. Examples of including someone in the group or excluding someone from the group...

During the course of the game participants observe their group, writing down anything observed during the game that fits under the heading on their paper. Once the game is over, each member of each group tells the rest of the group the heading on his/her paper and the observations that s/he made.

Discussion Topics

1. Were there more negative or more positive comments made during your game? Why do you feel this occurred?
2. Do you feel that you hear more negative or more positive comments in your daily life? Why do you think this occurs?
3. How do you feel when you hear negative comments? When you say negative comments?
4. How do you feel when you hear positive comments? When you say positive comments?
5. How can you learn to make positive comments rather than negative comments? How can you help those in your daily life to do the same?

AWARDS AND TROPHIES

Gaining a little insight into how others see us, especially knowing about their positive feelings toward us, is a step toward feeling better about ourselves. This activity gives group members a chance to make an award or trophy for someone else in the group to tell him/her some the good things they see in each other.

Everyone gets an award which will let them know what someone else sees in them. The best part about the activity is that each person can say something nice about someone else in a non-threatening way.

Objective

To communicate feelings to others by using symbols and to increase self-esteem by receiving positive comments from others.

Who

People with low self-esteem.
People who have trouble giving compliments.
The group should be familiar with each other.

Group Size

2 or more

Materials

- A pile of old newspapers
- Blank sheets of white and colored paper
- Marking pens
- Decorating materials (glitter, ribbon, stencils, water colors, etc.)
- Scissors, tape, glue

Description

Lay out all of the materials for the group to use. Assign each member of the group another group member to make an certificate or trophy for. The award should reflect something special or positive about the recipient.

Have each individual make an award by using the newspaper, paper and other tools. They can make a trophy in a form that represents the positive aspects of the individual or a certificate listing some outstanding characteristic or deed.

When each person is finished creating an award, hold an award ceremony. Allow each person to present his/her award to the person for whom s/he made it, along with an explanation of the creation and its meaning.

Discussion Topics

1. Was it easier or harder to tell someone how you felt about them without words? Why?
2. Is it easier to tell others something special about them or is it easier to have someone tell you something special about you?
3. How important is it to your self-esteem for others to say positive things about you?
4. How do you feel when you compliment others?
5. Name some ways you can express your feelings to others without needing to talk to them.
6. When would it be an advantage to communicate indirectly?

Variations

➲ If the group is small let each person make an award for more than one group member.
➲ Have each person also create an award that represents his/her own individual positive traits.

MiRROR

When we look in a mirror, we may not see ourselves the same way that other people see us. Often we see the negative parts, what we don't like about ourselves, how we fail to do what we think we should do. We may simply fail to see the good in ourselves that others see in us.

This activity is one of self-reflection. Are we too hard on ourselves? Do we ever pay attention to our good qualities? When people realize how hard they are on themselves, maybe they can ease up and start to realize the good qualities that they possess. Perhaps they will even feel better about themselves.

Objective

To explore how group members view themselves and to compare this perception to how they are viewed by others in the group. To increase self-esteem by receiving positive affirmations from others in the group and to recognize the origins of one's own self-esteem.

Who

People who have low self-esteem and/or negative self-perception. The group members should be familiar with each other.

Group Size

1 or more

Materials

- ➲ Blank sheets of paper
- ➲ Rulers
- ➲ Colored markers
- ➲ Pens, pencils

Description

Give each group member a blank piece of paper. Have each person draw a mirror frame, leaving at least one inch of blank space around the outside. Everyone must put their names on the top of the pieces of paper and then write down words or sentences inside of the mirror frame that describes how they view themselves.

Once everyone has completed this task, have them all place their mirrors in a pile. Allow time for everyone to write positive comments for everyone else in the blank space on the outside of each of the mirrors in the group. These comments should reflect how each individual views the others in the group. Encourage the group to be positive.

Once everyone has finished this task, give everyone back their mirrors and allow time for them to read the comments prior to discussion time.

Discussion Topics

1. Is there a difference between how you view yourself and how others view you?
2. Are you surprised by what others see in you?
3. Why is it important to find positive aspects of your personality?
4. Where do you get your self-esteem?

Variations

➲ If the group is large, break the group into smaller groups when it is time to write on the mirrors.
➲ If the group is young children or low functioning, provide an outline of a mirror frame for them to color in, rather than allowing them to create their own frame.
➲ Based upon the type of group, it may be appropriate to allow group members to write down anything, not only positive comments.
➲ Don't emphasize the fact that the comments written about others should be positive. This gives people with a low self-esteem more faith in what was written about them rather than assuming people wrote positive comments because they had too.

LABEL ME

People often think that they know all about you because of something they have heard or because of the way you look, as though there were labels on you. These labels often determine how we treat other people and how other people treat us. Think of what happens when the wrong label is put on a person. It can leave him/her feeling frustrated, like s/he hasn't had a fair chance.

This activity shows what it feels like to be labeled. Recognizing the effects of putting labels on people is a step towards getting rid of the negative labels we use for ourselves and others.

Objective

To increase group awareness of how people are treated by others and help people to recognize the positive and/or negative effects of actions and reactions of their peers towards them. To determine how people would like to be treated.

Who

People who feel they have been unfairly labeled.
People who are quick to judge other people based upon what they see or hear.

Group Size

4 or more

Materials

➲ Marking pen
➲ Tape
➲ Squares of paper with a stereotype or label on it
➲ Label ideas:
    Ignore me.
    I'm popular.
    I don't speak English.

I'm your best friend.
I act like I know everything.
Compliment me a lot.
I'm a nerd.
Laugh at my mistakes.
I'm stuck up.
I get on your nerves.
Listen to me carefully.
I give it my all.
Everyone wants to be like me.
Group bully.

Description

Tape a label on the back of each person in the group so that all of the others can see it. (See above for label ideas.) Tell the group to treat each person the way they would if the label were true. Be sure that nobody tells anybody else what label is posted on their back.

Once the labels are on, engage the group in an activity or game (i.e. volleyball, cards, basketball, an art project, croquet, etc.) so that interaction can take place while the labels are on. At the end of the game, have each person try to guess what label was on his/her back and talk about how it felt to be treated as s/he was during this activity.

Discussion Topics

1. What feelings do you have about how you were treated during this activity?
2. What label do you feel peers or society has given you?
3. Do you feel that others see you as you really are?
4. Do others treat you the way that you want to be treated?
5. How do you treat others who are different from you?
6. Why do we put labels on others and how do you feel about this?

GREAT GREETING CARDS

Saying nice things about people isn't always a very easy thing to do and saying nice things about yourself can be even harder. Greeting cards can make it easier for people to say positive things and to let other people know how they feel. By creating original greeting cards for themselves and for others, members of the group will have the opportunity to hear nice things twice.

Objective

To increase self-esteem through the act of complimenting others.
To increase self-esteem by recognizing one's own positive traits and acknowledging these traits.

Who

People with low self-esteem.
People who need to practice affirming other people.

Group Size

2 or more

Materials

- ➲ White paper
- ➲ Envelopes
- ➲ Markers
- ➲ Optional: water colors, tempera paints, glitter, glue, postage stamps

Description

Supply the group with enough materials to make two greeting cards each. Assign each person another member of the group. Each person makes two original greeting cards, one for the person s/he was assigned and another card for him/herself.

Each card must contain a positive message of praise or encouragement in it. The card for someone else will be passed on to the recipient at the end of the group session. The cards made by each of the people for themselves will be put in self-addressed envelopes and then given to the leader, who will mail the cards at a later date. If mailing the cards is not an option, allow them to keep their own cards.

Discussion Topics

1. Was it easier to make a card for someone else or for yourself? Why?
2. How did you feel after reading the card that someone made for you?
3. Did anyone have the same message in the card from someone else as in the card from yourself?

NEW NEWSPAPER

The newspapers these days are filled with a lot of bad news and many sad stories. By simply rearranging a few words, a negative newspaper headline can be turned into a positive one. Sharing the good news of our own lives is a great way to build confidence and improve self-esteem.

Objective

For people to identify positive qualities in themselves and positive events in their lives.

Who

People with low self-esteem.
People who need to recognize positive traits that they posses.

Group Size

1 or more

Materials

- ◗ Stack of old newspapers
- ◗ Glue
- ◗ Scissors
- ◗ Blank paper

Description

Each person creates a newspaper page about him/herself, by cutting out words from old newspapers and arranging these words into new headlines. The new headlines should be positive messages about the individual, describing what s/he likes about him/herself. Once everyone has created a "new newspaper", allow time for each person to read what s/he has created to the rest of the group.

Discussion Topics

1. Did you find it easy to write good news about yourself?
2. How did you feel when you read your "new newspaper" to the rest of the group?

Variations

➲ Have the members of the group make newspapers about other members of the group or about the group as a whole.
➲ Have the group make up headlines that describe things the way they would like them to be.
➲ Write stories to go with the headlines.

FANTASTIC FRAMES

Picture frames are used to display and even enhance great works of art. Sometimes it helps us to think of ourselves as a work of art. We can create ourselves that way if we choose. In this activity the frames display the best qualities in each of us for all to see.

Objective

To provide an opportunity for people to recognize their unique, individual positive traits and to share these traits verbally with the group.

Who

People who need to recognize that they have good traits and that the good traits are worth emphasizing.

Group Size

1 or more

Materials

- 5x7 or 8x10 blank cardboard picture frames
  or
- Frames cut from tag board in any size and shape
- Scissors
- Glue
- Markers
- Blank paper
- Anything else in your art supplies that would be good to use for frame decorations (i.e. ribbons, glitter, lace, colored paper, dried flowers, beads, sequins, etc.)

Description

Supply each person with a blank frame or piece of tag board, from which a frame can be cut. Provide time for group members to freely decorate their frames, being as creative as they wish. Once they are finished decorating the frames, each person writes down on a piece of paper at least three positive things that s/he like about him/herself, to display in the newly decorated frames.

Gather the group together once everyone has finished, allowing each person the chance to show his/her frame to the group and to share the positive things that s/he wrote.

Discussion Topics

1. Was it easy or hard for you to think of three positive things about yourself? Why?
2. How did it feel to write positive things about yourself?
3. Did everyone find the best things to include in his/her frame? What other positive things would you add?
4. How can you emphasize your good traits more in your everyday life?

COMPLIMENT COLLAGE

Sometimes it is difficult to express our feelings in words. Making collages of pictures is a popular way to express feelings and thoughts when it may not be easy to use words.

In this activity each group member gets to show how s/he feels about another member of the group by making a collage of his/her good qualities.

Objective

To increase one's self-esteem through the act of giving to others and by receiving positive comments from others.

Who

People who need to learn ways to express their feelings about other people.
People with low self-esteem.
Group members should be familiar with each other.

Group Size

2 or more

Materials

- Blank paper
- A stack of old magazines
- Glue
- Scissors
- Slips of paper
- Pens, pencils

Description

Write down the name of each person on a slip of paper and allow everyone to draw a name. Instruct the group that they are to create a collage using magazine pictures that represent the good qualities of the person whose name they have selected.

The pictures should be glued to a piece of paper in a collage manner. Once everyone has finished, allow them to share what they have created with the group and explain their collage while giving it to the individual that it represents.

Discussion Topics

1. Is it always easy to find good traits in other people? Why?
2. How did you feel when you were saying good things about someone else?
3. Was it easier to express yourself with pictures or with words?
4. How did you feel when people were saying good things about you?

NEGATiVE COMMENT LiST

A sarcastic comment that is meant to be funny can actually be very hurtful for some. These comments, as well as any obvious negative comments or put-downs, can have a devastating effect on people. Sometimes people do not even realize that they are saying these types of things unless it is brought to their attention.

This game is a non-threatening and fun way to help the group recognize its negative behavior. Knowing that it's there is the first step toward changing it.

Objective

For group members to observe how many negative comments are made during an activity and to be able to recognize what types of comments have a negative effect on others.

Who

People who put other people down, perhaps without realizing how damaging it can be.
People who have low self-esteem as a result of hearing many negative comments.

Group Size

2 or more

Materials

➲ Paper
➲ Pen or pencil
➲ Various game supplies

Description

Set up an interactive game for the group to play (i.e. cards, board game, sports, active game, etc.). Inform the group that during the game all negative comments will be written down. The leader may keep track of the comments or assign a member of the group the job of recording negative comments. Once the activity is over, gather the group together and read the list of negative comments.

Discussion Topics

1. Do you think that all of the comments were bad or were some in "good fun"?
2. When is a comment simply sarcastic rather than negative?
3. Has there ever been a time when you said a negative comment that really hurt someone else's feelings? Did you feel good or bad and why?
4. Has there ever been a time when others have really hurt you with what they said? What did you do about it?
5. What is the best way to handle a negative comment?
6. Would it be a good idea to make fewer negative comments? What effect would this have on you or on others?

Variations

➲ Use a large sheet of paper, black board or dry erase board with a marker. Any group member may record a negative comment made during the game?
➲ Secretly write down negative comments made during an interactive game, letting the group know afterwards that you made a list and read the list to the group.

THE UNEXPECTED GIFT

Giving gifts to others is a positive experience for both the giver and the receiver. The person who receives the gift feels appreciated and recognized. The giver knows that s/he has done something to make someone else feel better. When gifts are given for no reason, the feelings are more significant and special.

This activity reminds group members of the value of giving to others and lets them feel the sense of self-worth and good feelings that come from giving.

Objective

To increase self-esteem in people by encouraging them to give to others without expecting anything in return.

Who

People who have difficulty focusing on others rather than on themselves.

Group Size

1 or more

Materials

➲ Any arts and crafts supplies available

Description

Each person in the group makes a gift for someone else for no special occasion. If there is another group in the facility (i.e. an adult group, children's group, staff), you may wish to assign each group member to a specific person in that group and ask the group members to make special gifts for them. Another option is to assign each person a different member of the group to receive his/her gift. Or allow each person to chose anyone they know to make a special something for.

After the gifts are created, present the gifts to those for whom they were made, as a group, individually or in an anonymous manner. Chose the most appropriate way for your group.

Discussion Topics

1. How did it feel to give without getting something in return?
2. Do you usually expect something (even a "thank you") in return, when you do something for someone else? Why or why not?
3. What benefit could you receive by giving to (or helping) others?
4. Can you think of some people in need to whom you could give a gift? What could you do for them?

NOT COOL (BUT POSSIBLY FUN)

Being influenced by others is a large part of growing up. Peer pressure can keep us from doing things that we want to do and force us into doing things that we don't want to do. It is important to understand that is okay to be our own selves, especially when it is in our own best interest.

Embarrassment is a big part of peer pressure, so we are going to play some very goofy games in very silly ways just to give everyone a chance to be totally embarrassed. That way the people in the group can start to recognize how their actions or lack of actions are influenced by what others think and do.

Objective

To increase understanding of the influence peer pressure has on how an individual chooses to act. To increase self-esteem by showing the ability to be comfortable with one's own self when others are present.

Who

People who don't have enough confidence in themselves to do something that their friends don't approve of.

Group Size

4 or more

Materials

- ➲ A large bag of old and very stupid looking clothes
- ➲ Game directions for one of the following four games
- ➲ Game equipment varies

Description

Fill a large bag with old clothes, hats, ties, etc. Pass the bag around and, without looking into the bag, each participant must pick out an article of clothing and put it on. Continue to pass the bag around until it is empty. Once everyone is dressed and looking a bit silly, play some very goofy games. (Some suggestions are on the following pages).

Discussion Topics

1. How did you feel during this activity and why did you feel that way?
2. Did you have fun? Why or why not?
3. Do you have a group of friends with whom you would have felt more comfortable playing these games? A group with whom you would have been less comfortable? Why?
4. When do others influence your actions? Is this good or bad? Why?
5. What can you do to feel comfortable with who you are, no matter who you are with?

QUARTER DROP

Objective

A goofy game to use with *NOT COOL (BUT POSSIBLY FUN)*

Group Size

4 or more

Materials

➲ Two paper cups
➲ Two quarters

Description

Divide the group into two teams. Each team forms a line, one behind the other, facing a paper cup that is placed at the other end of the room, with the open end up. The first person in each line is given a quarter, which s/he must place between the knees.

Give the signal to "go" to start the race. Each person tries to get the quarter into the team cup by carrying it to the cup, holding it between his/her knees. Still using only the knees, the person drops the quarter into the cup. If the quarter is dropped between the start line and the cup, the person may pick it up and put it back between the knees.

After dropping the quarter into the cup, the person picks it up and runs back to the next person in line. That person puts the quarter between his/her knees and then carries it to the cup. Continue until everyone gets a turn to drop the quarter into the cup.

ORANGE PASS RELAY

Objective

A goofy game to use with NOT COOL (BUT POSSIBLY FUN)

Group Size

8 or more

Materials

➲ Two oranges

Description

Divide the group into two teams and line each team up single file. The first person in each line is given an orange that s/he holds under his/her chin. The orange is then passed to the next person in line who grabs it with his/her chin and chest. The process continues until the orange reaches the end of the line.

If the orange is dropped at any time, it may be picked up and placed back under the chin of the person who dropped it and passed on down the line to the end.

MARSHMALLOW FiND

Objective

A goofy game to use with NOT COOL (BUT POSSiBLY FUN)

Group Size

4 or more

Materials

- ⊃ Two pie pans
- ⊃ Five pound bag of flour
- ⊃ Bag of mini marshmallows
- ⊃ Toothpick for each participant

Description

Divide the group into two teams and give each person a toothpick. Line up each team single file, facing a pie pan full of flour with mini marshmallows buried in it.

Give the "go" signal. The first person in each line goes to the pie pan with a toothpick in his/her mouth and must find a marshmallow in the pan by using only the tooth pick. No hands allowed. Once a marshmallow is found, the next person in the line does the same, until everyone has found a marshmallow.

SPUD SWING

Objective

A goofy game to use with NOT COOL (BUT POSSIBLY FUN)

Group Size

4 or more

Materials

- Ladies nylons (new or used) 1 pair for every 2 participants
- One potato per person
- Two golf balls
- Two paper cups

Description

Cut each pair of nylons in half to separate the two legs and drop a spud down to the toe of each one. Give each participant a "potato leg" to tie around his/her waist so the spud hangs down behind each person to the floor and between the legs.

Once everyone has their "potato leg" ready, divide the group into two teams lined up single file. Set up each team facing a cup that is across the floor, about ten feet away, with the open end facing the team. Give the person in the front of each line a golf ball, which they must then hit into their team's cup by swinging their hips to hit the ball with the potato. Once the ball goes into the cup, it may be picked up and run back to the next person in line who then attempts to get the ball into the cup in the same way. This continues until everyone has a turn to do the "spud swing."

SOMEONE WHO... BiNGO

Some people can't name anything that they like about themselves or that they are good at, but when they are asked specific questions, the response may be different. By turning questions of self-worth into a Bingo game, maybe everyone will see some positive traits in themselves and others that they would not recognize otherwise.

Objective

To recognize and acknowledge individual positive traits of each of the group members.

Who

People who have difficulty recognizing positive traits in themselves.

Group Size

5 or more

Materials

- ⊃ SOMEONE WHO... BiNGO cards (copy from the page after the activity)
- ⊃ Pens, pencils
- ⊃ Optional: prizes for those who get a "bingo"

Description

Give everyone in the group a SOMEONE WHO... BiNGO card and a pen or pencil. Each square has a statement in it that describes positive qualities that a person may possess. The object is to acquire signatures from the other group members in order to fill up the bingo card and to claim a "bingo" with five in a row or a "blackout" when all the squares are filled up with signatures.

When seeking signatures, the questions must be asked "Are you someone who...?" If the person's response to the question is yes, s/he signs in that square. When seeking signatures, the seeker may only ask someone two questions before they must move on to someone else. Once someone has signed a bingo card, s/he may not sign it again (depending on group size, signing more than once may be allowed).

At the end of the game, but prior to the group discussion, gather the group together, read each square out loud and ask for a show of hands of anyone who signed that particular square.

Discussion Topics

1. Do you feel that you have a lot of good qualities? Why or why not?
2. Why is it important to find positive qualities in yourself? In others?
3. Is there anyone that you approached who said "no" to one of your "Are you someone who..." questions that you felt should have said yes? If so, who and why?

Variations

➲ Create an original Bingo card to fit the needs of the group.
➲ Play blackout with a large group.

Someone Who... Bingo

Someone who has a good sense of humor	Someone who is smart	Someone who is a good leader	Someone who does nice things for others	Someone who is a good sister or brother
Someone who is musically talented	Someone who feels that others enjoy being around them	Someone who is creative	Someone who is helpful to others	Someone who can be trusted by others
Someone who is excited about the future	Someone who is a good listener	Someone who is caring toward others	Someone who others want to be around	Someone who is confident with who they are
Someone who is good at sports	Someone who would make a good friend	Someone who likes their own smile	Someone who is good at arts and crafts	Someone who is happy with how much they weigh
Someone who has good sportsman-ship	Someone who communi-cates clearly	Someone who is a good cook	Someone who is a hard worker	Someone who is happy with the way they look

THE WRECKING YARD

SELF-DISCOVERY

The end of the school year was always exciting and fun. My favorite part of school ending was getting my yearbook. Being quiet and somewhat shy, I didn't talk a lot about myself and I didn't really know what others knew of me or thought about me, even though I always had many friends. Once I had my yearbook in my hands, I would have all my friends sign it. I was always eager to come home in the afternoon, sit on my bed in my room and read what others had written to me. I learned how others saw me, what was special about me and who felt close to me. Sitting alone in my room with my yearbook filled with compliments, special notes and bonds of friendship was a form of self-discovery for me that I very much enjoyed.

Learning how others see us and discovering how we see ourselves, is an eye-opening experience that can help us grow and change into a better people. A yearly evaluation at work, an intimate talk with a close friend, receiving a special letter from a loved one and writing in a journal are all ways of discovering more about ourselves.

Self-discovery is one step in the therapeutic process that is very important. A large part of successful therapy is helping people realize what they do, what they need to change and what they can do to make that change. A group setting is a wonderful opportunity for group members to learn more about themselves in order to move through the process of change. When group members share their feelings and share what they see in themselves and in each other, they learn new insights into their own behaviors and realize how these behaviors affect their own lives and the lives of those around them.

Sitting around in a group and talking is one way for people to share their feelings and give others feedback about what they have observed.

Sometimes it is difficult to get young people to talk in this type of setting but when the opportunity to talk about feelings is presented in the process of a game, youth will often open up much more easily, sometimes without even realizing that they are. In this chapter there are many games and activities that offer the opportunity of self-discovery.

SELF-DISCOVERY ACTIVITIES

GOAL GROUP

Growing and changing is an important part of bettering yourself. Setting positive, reachable goals is a way to feel in control of making a step forward.

Having a weekly goal group gives group members a chance to set their own goals and support each other in the progress that they are making. They will have a feeling of control over the progress that they making, giving them self-confidence and a sense of accomplishment that they can carry with them in the future.

Objective

For participants to set individual goals to work towards during their time with the group. To determine the progress in meeting these individual goals. To provide an opportunity for group members to hold each other accountable in working towards individual goals.

Who

People who are working to better their lives.

Group Size

2 or more

Materials

➲ Blank 3x5 cards
➲ Spiral notebook
➲ Pens, pencils

Description

Gather the group together and ask each individual to state a goal that s/he will be committed to during his/her time with the group. When an individual has stated a goal, ask the rest of the group if they have any feedback to give to the individual about the goal. Ask the group if they feel the goal is reasonable for the individual. If someone cannot think of a goal, give that person the opportunity to ask the group for help in determining a reasonable goal for him/her to work towards during time with the group.

The goals should reflect the issues that each person is attempting to work out while with the group. Once a goal is determined for an individual, write it down on a 3x5 card for him/her to keep as a reminder throughout the week. The group leader should use the spiral notebook to write down each goal and to keep as a reference. If you are in a treatment facility that has a treatment plan for each individual, put the goal in the treatment plan as a part of his/her therapy. This is a great way to give patients control over their own treatment and to let them take responsibility for their own actions.

On a weekly or monthly basis hold a "goal group," to determine the progress that people are making towards the goals that they have set for themselves. Ask each individual to state their goal to the group and the progress that they have made towards reaching that goal. Once an individual states the goal that s/he has been working towards and states the progress that has been made towards his/her own goal, offer the opportunity for others in the group to give feedback about the progress that they have seen in that individual throughout the week. This is an opportunity to revise, resolve or add to any of the goals. If there is a new member to the group, this activity is a chance for the individual to come up with a goal to work towards when with the group.

Discussion Topics

Discuss the goals and progress as described in the description section.

SENTIMENTAL SONGS

The words and music of a song can evoke many different feelings. This activity allows each group member to put some of those feelings into a picture and then share the picture with the other people in the group. This is a great activity for getting reserved people to share some of the feelings that they normally keep hidden inside.

Objective

To allow people to explore their own feelings about music and freely express their feelings through music.

Who

People who have difficulty expressing their feelings verbally.

Group Size

1 or more

Materials

- ➲ Recording of any song that contains meaningful words
- ➲ Stereo
- ➲ Paper
- ➲ Paint, brushes, water
- ➲ Colored markers

Description

Set up the tables so that each person can work independently, without being influenced by others. Supply each person with paper and paint or markers. Prior to starting the song, instruct the group that while listening to the song, everyone is to create a picture based upon how the song makes him/her feel. If the song has a strong message, I often ask the group members to paint something specific using the song as a metaphor for the path that their life has taken. For example, when I use a song about a river,

I ask the group members to paint a river that is representative of their own lives.

Play the song two or three times. If more time is needed, you may wish to play an assortment of songs with the same theme or some soft instrumental music for the remaining time. Afterwards allow time for each person to share his/her art work with the group, explaining its meaning and significance.

Discussion Topics

1. Why did you paint what you painted?
2. What did you learn about yourself as a result of this activity?
3. What did you learn about others as a result of this activity?
4. How can music be used in dealing with feelings and emotions?

Variations

➲ Make a clay sculpture instead of painting or drawing.

THE SONG AND I

Expressing yourself through music is a non-threatening way to let others know how you feel. That is why there are so many songs written about feelings or dedicated to those we love on the radio.

This activity allows group members to select a song that represents how they are feeling and to lead a discussion about those feelings with the rest of the group.

Objective

To explore the use of music as a way of expressing feelings.

Who

People who have difficulty expressing their feelings.

Group Size

1 or more

Materials

- A prerecorded tape of four to six very different songs
- Stereo
- One large sheet of paper per song
- Markers

Description

Prior to the activity make a recording of four to six different types of songs. (I like to select a soft instrumental song, a fun beach song, loud rock and a popular song.) Always make sure the words and music suggest a particular mood.

Once the group is gathered together, explain that you will be playing a variety of music selections for them. Ask the group to listen to the music and for each member of the group to select the song which most reflects his/her mood at that time (not simply the song that they like the best).

After playing the tape once, play it again, but this time supply a large sheet of paper and markers for each song and place them in different spots around the room. During the second playing of the songs, ask participants go to the designated sheet of paper for the song they feel most reflects their mood at that time. On the sheet of paper designated for their song, instruct the group members to write down how the song makes them feel and the mood that it represents for them.

Once all the songs have played through, allow time for each of the song groups to talk among themselves about why they chose that song. Gather the song groups back together and have each of them read their paper to the rest of the group and share what they talked about.

Discussion Topics

1. Did everyone in your group generally feel the same about the song as you did?
2. Did anyone feel differently about any of the songs than what the group wrote down about it?
3. Can different music affect your mood? How?
4. What does the music that we choose to listen to say about us, if anything?
5. What connection is there between music and emotions that we feel, if any?
6. Can we use music to help us at all? If so how?

HOW I SEE YOU, HOW YOU SEE ME

We always wonder how we are perceived by others, but it is really hard to be sure. Giving ourselves a chance to see how others perceive us, gives us a chance to look at ourselves from another viewpoint.

Choosing a symbol to represent ourselves and others is a different way to share who we are, to see how someone else perceives us and to tell others how we feel about them in a fun, yet, non-threatening way.

Objective

For each person to compare the way they perceive themselves with the way other people perceive them.

Who

People who have difficulty talking about the way they feel.
People who have the ability to be insightful.
Group members who are familiar with each other.

Group Size

2 or more

Materials

➲ None

Description

Gather the group together and assign each person to another member of the group and ask each group member to find an object that they feel is symbolic of that person. The symbolic object may be found inside or outside wherever the group might be. At the same time each person should also find an object to symbolize him/herself.

The symbol may be something tangible, such as a flower, or intangible, such as a cloud in the sky overhead. Give the group an area that they may go to find their symbolic objects or go for a walk as a group. This activity may be done in a building, but is best if done outside in a park-like setting.

Once everyone has gathered a symbolic object, bring the group together so that everyone has the chance to share their personal symbol and explain its meaning to the rest of the group. After each person shares his/her personal symbol, have the person who collected a symbol for the person share what s/he collected. There may be a discussion after each explanation, so the person receiving the symbol may agree, disagree or ask questions regarding the symbol.

Discussion Topics

1. Did you find a symbol that really represented how you see yourself?
2. Was it easier to explain your feelings with the symbol than it would have been without the symbol?
3. Were you surprised by the symbol chosen for you? Why or why not?
4. How well did the symbol chosen by the other person match with your perception of who you are?
5. Was it be easier or harder to find a symbol for yourself?
6. What did you learn about yourself or about anyone else in the group as a result of this activity?

Variations

➲ Specify what quality of the individual the symbol should represent (i.e. positive traits).
➲ Just find one symbol, either the symbol for him/herself or the symbol for the other person.

SITUATION IMITATION

Bad habits and negative behaviors are hard to change. They are even harder to change when you don't even notice what you are doing. This activity helps group members (and the group leader) recognize their own behaviors and encourages them to change for the better.

Objective

To give group members the opportunity to confront their peers and help them recognize their negative behaviors. To help people recognize their own negative behaviors and to recognize how these can be changed to positive behaviors.

Who

People who display negative behaviors and who need to recognize what these behaviors are.

Group Size

4 or more

Materials

- ➲ Paper
- ➲ Pens, pencils
- ➲ Paper sack
- ➲ Various game equipment

Description

Write down each participant's name on a piece of paper, including all the names of the group leaders participating in the activity. Put all the names into the paper sack so that each participant can draw out the name of another group member without revealing the name to others.

Once the names are selected, instruct the group that they will be playing a fun game while at the same time imitating the individual whose name they have drawn. Instruct the group members to act the way that they feel this person acts, talks and behaves during a typical group game or activity. The game played may be anything from a table game to an outdoor running game. This activity can be fun and very revealing to all those involved. Depending on the group, limits may need to be set prior to the activity.

Discussion Topics

1. Do you feel that you were accurately portrayed? Why or why not?
2. What behavior from your imitator did you not like or like? Why?
3. Why do you think your imitator emphasized the actions and behaviors that s/he did?
4. How can you change any of your negative behaviors? How can you emphasize your positive behaviors?
5. Did the person imitating the group leader do a good job?

HATS

Throughout our lives we will wear many different "hats" as we take on many different roles. By recognizing what hats we have to wear and the roles that others think we have, we can learn more about ourselves and become more aware of how we fit into the big picture.

This activity lets group members choose a hat for themselves to represent how they are feeling today. Then they get to create a hat for someone else to show how they perceive that person.

Objective

For people to share feelings of self-perception to the group and for each individual to learn how s/he is perceived by a peer.

Who

Group members who are familiar with each other.

Group Size

2 or more

Materials

- ◔ Newspaper or butcher paper
- ◔ Tape
- ◔ Colored markers

Description

Each person is assigned another member of the group and is instructed to make a paper hat for that person. Each participant makes a hat for him/herself and for the individual to whom s/he has been assigned. The hats should be colored in a way to create a type of hat which symbolically represents the person it is for (i.e. colored like a ski cap for someone who is "warm to all those around him/her" or a chef's hat for someone who "takes all the small things in life and brings them together to make great things"). Encourage people to be creative.

When the hats are finished, hold a "ceremony" in which everyone has a chance to explain their own hats and to present the other hat to the individual for whom it was created. This activity should be done with a group of participants that have been together long enough to know each other well.

Discussion Topics

1. What do you think about the hat that was created for you?
2. How did you decide what kind of hat to create for yourself?
3. How many different hats do you wear in your life?
4. Do you have any hats that you wear in your life that you would like to change? If so, what are they and why do you wish to change them?

TO MAKE THiS ßOX REPRESENT ME, I WOULD...

Being able to open up to others in a group is the first step in becoming an active member of the group. Some people have difficulty opening up to others and sharing their feelings. Something as simple as a cardboard box can be a helpful tool for getting people to feel comfortable about sharing their feelings with the group, for the first time or even for the fifteenth time.

Objective

To learn the perception that each person in the group holds about him/herself. To provide a chance for people to open up to others in the group.

Who

People who have difficulty expressing their feelings directly.

Group Size

2 or more

Materials

➲ An empty box with a lid

Description

Gather the group into a circle. The leader holds the empty box and says "to make this box represent me I would..." (i.e. "I would fill it with chocolate covered candy and then tape it shut because it is difficult to find out what is inside of me but once I open up there are many wonderful surprises to be discovered.").

Once the leader has completed the statement, s/he passes the box to the next person who then completes the sentence and then passes it to the

person beside him/her. The box continues around the circle until everyone
has had a turn.

Discussion Topics

1. Did the box make it easier to say something?
2. Did you feel that you could be in better control of how much you said?
3. How did it feel to learn about the box that represented other people?

Variations

➔ Change what the box represents: "To make this box represent
_____ (my family, the way I deal with my anger, my relationship
with God, my role in this group, etc.), I would..."

FAMiLY SCULPTURES

How we relate to our families and how they relate to us is a very important part of who we are. By making "sculptures" of our families, others can learn more about the situations we grew up in and live in. This information can help people to understand each other better. It can also make it easier to talk about good things and bad things that are happening in each person's family.

Objective

To provide a non-threatening setting for people to share their family dynamics with the rest of the group. To open the door for future discussions concerning family relationships.

Who

People who have difficulty talking about their families.

Group Size

6 or more

Materials

➲ None

Description

Allow one individual at a time to "sculpt" a picture of his/her family, using the other members of the group to pose as family members. The individual should select any group member to represent a family member who has similar traits, if possible. The family "sculpture" should be still and each person should be placed in a particular position or distance from the others based upon the family member that they are representing and this individual's relation to the rest of the family. The individual making the sculpture should place him/herself in it as well, to represent his/her relationship to the rest of the family.

Once the "sculpture" has been completed, an explanation is given by the person who created it so that the group will understand what the "sculpture" represents.

HINT: It is a good idea to allow one of the leaders of the group to "sculpt" his/her family first as an example and so the activity is less threatening to the group.

Discussion Topics

1. Could you make a good representation of your family with the people in the group?
2. What changes in the sculpture would make your life better?
2. How did it feel to be part of someone else's family?

Variations

- ➲ Allow the "sculpture" to move as directed by the sculptor to represent changes that occurred as s/he was growing up.
- ➲ After the sculpture is made, have the person change the sculpture to represent how they would like it to be.
- ➲ The sculptor may chose another group member to represent him/her.

HUMAN SCULPTURES

How we are perceived by others is often very different from how we view ourselves. By learning how others see us, we can determine how others interpret what we say and do.

This activity gives group members a chance to recognize things that they may want to change about themselves by taking a look at their lives through the eyes of the other members of the group.

Objective

To encourage inner growth of people in the group by providing them with the opportunity to learn how they are perceived by others and asking them to compare this perception to how they view their own life.

Who

People who have trouble recognizing how their words and actions are perceived by others.
Group members who are familiar with each other.

Group Size

2 or more

Materials

➲ None

Description

Gather the group in a circle and ask for a volunteer to stand in the middle of the circle. The person in the center now becomes the "clay" to be molded by the rest of the group members. Those in the circle work together, moving the "clay" into a position which they feel is representative of the person in the center of the circle (i.e. the "clay" may be molded into a running position to represent someone who is running away from his/her problems).

Once the "clay" has been molded, the group explains its creation to the person who is the "clay." Do this for each member of the group. The "clay" may be molded into more than one position if the group thinks of more than one sculpture to represent that person.

Discussion Topics

1. Do you feel that you were portrayed accurately? Why or why not?
2. Are you surprised at the way that your peers view your life? Why?
3. Is it easier to analyze someone else or to analyze yourself? Why?

Variations

➲ This may be done in pairs and then each pair will explain their sculptures of each other to the rest of the group.

MUSIC MEDLEY

If you ask people who are depressed what kind of music they like to listen to, they will often name a band or song that is sad and negative. People who are angry often name bands and songs that are about killing and destruction. While it isn't always true, there is a clear connection.

Music is something that can evoke strong emotions, bring up memories and bring people together. By listening to a wide variety of music, the group can have a discussion about the role music plays in people's lives and the positive or negative effects music can have on them.

Objective

For people to come to an understanding of how the music that they listen to may have an effect on how they feel. To learn what emotions and feelings different types of music evoke and explore the reasons for these feelings.

Who

People who listen to music.

Group Size

1 or more

Materials

- ➲ Create a tape containing clips of music broken up into classifications, with a noticeable pause between each one (i.e. country, jazz, top 40, classical, rap, heavy metal, etc.)
- ➲ Tape player
- ➲ Paper
- ➲ Drawing supplies
- ➲ Pens, pencils

Description

Supply each person with several sheets of paper, drawing and writing supplies. Instruct the group to listen to each section of the tape carefully and to write down words or draw pictures which represent any feelings that the music evokes in them.

Once there is a break in the music, each person should use a new piece of paper or a different section of the piece of paper they are already using, to distinguish the different feelings that various types of music brings to them.

Discussion Topics

1. Which types of music gave you positive feelings? Which types gave you negative feelings? Why?
2. How does peer pressure determine the type of music you and your friends chose to listen to?
3. Do you feel that the type of music we listen to affects us emotionally? Does it make a statement about a person's personality?
4. How can music be used in dealing with feelings and emotions?
5. Why is it important to understand how music can affect us?

Variations

➲ Use one large piece of paper divided into sections so all members of a group may write on the same piece of paper and responses may be compared.

LAVISH LYRICS

Any group that has been together for a period of time begins to form a unique identity. By coming together and expressing this identity in a song, your group can establish what makes them unique and build a stronger bond in the process.

Objective

For people to work together, as a group, to create a song representative of the group. To encourage creativity and self-expression. To explore the use of music as a means of expressing feelings.

Who

Group members who are familiar with each other.

Group Size

2 or more

Materials

- ⮑ Stereo
- ⮑ A selected recording of a song
- ⮑ Paper
- ⮑ Pen or pencil

Description

Chose any song that is available on a tape or CD and obtain a copy of the words to the song if it is available. Give the group a time limit to come up with new lyrics to the song that the group members feel is reflective of the group. This activity seems to go better when group leaders let the group work without any leaders getting involved in the process.

Discussion Topics

1. Was this difficult or easy for the group? Why?
2. Why did the group choose the words that they did?
3. Was anyone surprised by any of the words or ideas that anyone in the group thought were representative of the group?
4. Do you think the words to the new song adequately represent the group or could more be added? If so, what?
5. What ways did you find of expressing your feelings?

Variations

➲ Supply a number of recordings and allow the group to choose the song.
➲ Play a song and let each individual create his/her own words for the song.

IF I WERE A FLOWER

Do you often wonder what others think about you? By finding out how others view us, we can come to a better understanding of who we really are. This game is a fun and entertaining way to explore what others see when they take a look at us.

Objective

To learn how others perceive us, so that we may come to a better understanding of who we are.

Who

Group members who are familiar with each other.

Group Size

4 or more

Materials

➲ None

Description

One person in the group leaves the room while the rest of the group selects a group member. The person out of the room must guess who was selected by asking specific questions about the person who was chosen. The questions asked must be as follows "If this person was a flower, what type of flower would s/he be?" Anything may be used in the place of the word "flower" to gain clues about who was selected.

Group members answer the question by selecting something in that category that they feel represents the person selected. For example "If this person was a type of ice cream what type of ice cream would s/he be?" Answer "bubble gum". The description should not reflect a physical description but rather represent internal qualities of that person.

Once the guesser (after asking many different questions) figures out who was selected, the one who was selected may ask his/her peers why certain answers were given. "Why did you say I was like bubble gum ice-cream?", "Because you are a bubbly fun person and have a very colorful personality." This game really helps participants learn what others see in them.

Discussion Topics

1. How accurate were the descriptions about you?
2. What new things did you learn about yourself as a result of this game?

Variations

➲ Someone sits in the middle of the circle. S/he points to someone in the circle and names a category. The person pointed to must say something from the category that represents the person in the center. This continues in a rapid manner until everyone has responded to a different category. Once the round is over, the person in the middle may ask anyone in the group why they gave a particular answer.

NEW ROLE

If we stay in our own comfort zone and do not challenge ourselves to go beyond these familiar walls, we cannot grow and change. When we take on a role that is new and uncomfortable, we have the chance to expand our comfort zone until things that once were difficult become easy and safe.

This activity gives group members a chance to try different ways of acting to see how it feels to act in a way that is normally uncomfortable for them. Change is often a scary thing at first but, with the right attitude and mind set, change can be a positive asset to everyone's life.

Objective

For people to learn how to take on an unfamiliar role in a group and to recognize their ability to change to become a better person.

Who

People who are stuck in their roles and have a difficult time moving out of them.

Group Size

3 or more

Materials

➲ Paper
➲ Pen or pencil

Description

During any game or group activity, assign each person a role to take on that is opposite of how s/he normally acts (i.e. assign a shy person a leadership or outgoing role). Give each person his/her role on a slip of paper, so that others in the group cannot see what it is. During the activity, all participants are to act the parts given to them instead of how they would normally act.

SOME ROLE SUGGESTIONS:
Only speak when asked a question.
Agree with everything.
Act as the group leader.
Disagree with everything.
You are happy with who you are.

Discussion Topics

1. How did you feel during this activity?
2. Was it difficult or easy for you to take on a new role in the group? Why?
3. Are there any roles that you take on in life that you would like to change?
4. How could you go about changing the roles that you take on in life?

UNiQUE QUALiTiES

Identifying unique qualities that we each possess is an important part of recognizing what makes us special and different from others. In this game, group members get to share some of their unique qualities with others and hear about the special qualities other people in the group have.

Objective

For people to recognize positive traits about themselves and to learn more about others in the group.

Who

Everyone.

Group Size

4 or more

Materials

➲ 3x5 index cards
➲ Paper
➲ Pens, pencils

Description

Each person writes down five unique qualities that they like about themselves on a 3x5 index card. Instruct them not to put their names on their cards and to return the cards to the leader when they are finished. The leader collects all of the cards and mixes them up before reading them to the group.

Each person tries to guess the identity of the person with those unique qualities and writes the answer on the paper. After reading the cards once through the leader reads the cards again. At this point people may verbally guess whose card is being read before the owner of the card admits to owning those unique qualities.

THE WRECKiNG YARD

Discussion Topics

1. What did you learn about the people in the group today?
2. Did you share something today that you haven't shared before?

Variations

➲ Give a prize to the person who was able to match the most people with their "unique qualities."

LEiSURE EDUCATiON

Skiing, hiking, kayaking, church youth group on the weekends. Soccer, student council and school on the weekdays. When I was a young, I didn't have time to get into trouble. I was very fortunate to have a wonderful family that did a lot of activities together. Many children and teenagers are not so fortunate, and they spend their free time doing things that are not healthy. As a therapist or counselor, it is very important to teach youth the importance of making good leisure choices and that the choices they make really do make a difference.

The first step in leisure education is to make people aware of their current leisure lifestyle. This can be done through worksheets, discussions, projects or even games. Many youth are unaware that how they spend their free time is unhealthy. When their family and friends spend most of their leisure time smoking, drinking and partying, they sometimes don't know how to do anything else. Or if they are very depressed and have a lot of free time to spend by themselves, with little support from family and friends, it is easy to become even more depressed. When children and teens become aware of how they spend their free time and recognize that it makes a difference in how they feel and act, this revelation can become a large part of changing to a healthier leisure lifestyle.

Once people recognize that they need to change the way that they spend their free time, teaching healthy, alternative ways of spending leisure time is the next step in leisure education. Making people aware of what recreational options they have and helping them to figure out a way to go about getting involved in these activities is the goal. In a group setting there is a good opportunity for discussion and sharing of ideas among the group members. Leisure education can be just as important to a therapy program as any other aspect and should not be overlooked.

If you need more help creating a complete leisure education program with an emphasis on why healthy leisure is important and how to make leisure healthier, see **Leisure Step Up**, by Dave Dehn (Idyll Arbor, Inc.).

LEISURE EDUCATION ACTIVITIES

LEISURE THEME COLLAGE

We often fill our free time with the same activities that we have done time and time again. We do what we are familiar with and, for this reason, most of us have only a handful of activities that we engage in when we have a moment of spare time.

One of the first steps to take towards changing people's leisure lifestyle is to show them the wide variety of things that they can do. In this activity we use the knowledge of the members of the group to create a large list of possible activities to participate in during leisure time.

Objective

To increase awareness of leisure activities that are available.

Who

People who need to change their current leisure lifestyle.

Group Size

2 or more

Materials

- Pile of old magazines
- Glue
- Scissors
- Paper

Description

Assign each group member one of the following topics:
- Activities to do with a family
- Activities to do with friends
- Activities to do alone
- Activities to do when the weather is bad
- Activities to do when the weather is good
- Activities to do on a vacation

○ Activities that don't cost any money
○ Activities that provide exercise
○ Activities to help you relax
○ Activities to help you release anger

Instruct the group members to use the old magazines to find pictures about the topic, cut these out and glue them to a piece of paper to make a collage.

Once everyone has completed their collage, allow time for sharing each individual collage. This is a good activity to learn about the leisure lifestyles of other people. If possible, assign topics according to issues that individuals may be dealing with (i.e. family, anger, etc.).

Discussion Topics

For each category:
1. Which of these activities do you do now? Which ones might you try in the future?
2. What other activities do each of you do?

At the end of the presentations:
1. Did you find any interesting new activities?
2. What other topics would you like to find activities for?

Variations

○ If group is large, assign specific topics to more than one person.
○ Allow members of the group to select their own categories.

TiME SWiTCH

Playing in the backyard with a bunch of other kids or hanging out in a friend's bedroom after school are examples of unstructured activities. Going to a church sponsored event, school dance or football practice fall into the category of structured activities.

Some people keep themselves out of trouble by becoming engaged in mainly structured activities while others enjoy the freedom found when engaging in unstructured activities. Helping the members of the group recognize the role that planned and unplanned activities play in their lives will help them make better choices in their leisure lifestyle.

Objective

For people to recognize behavior that is related to the use or misuse of their leisure time and to explore the difference between structured and unstructured time.

Who

People who could benefit from a more or less structured leisure lifestyle.

Group Size

4 or more

Materials

➲ Varies

Description

Divide the group time into two parts. Spend half of the group time playing a game that is organized and led by the leader of the group. This organized game may be anything from a board game to a running game, as long as it has rules and includes everyone in the group.

Once the group time is half way over, stop the organized game and allow the group to have unstructured free time. Provide the opportunity for

THE WRECKING YARD

free play, by providing materials and equipment that are available in the facility.

At the end of the group time, gather the group together and make a group list of the good and bad aspects of structured time and the good and bad aspects of unstructured time.

Discussion Topics

1. Do you ever find yourself getting into trouble when time is structured? Unstructured? If so why?
2. What are the benefits you receive when you are involved in structured activities?
3. Why is it important to be able to spend unstructured free time in a positive way?
4. If you feel you should be involved in more structured activities, how can you do that?

FAMILY ACTIVITY

Encouraging group members to plan and engage in family activities is a simple way for them to improve communications and build relations between family members.

The planned activities can be something simple such as a walk or as complicated as a week-long backpacking trip. Encourage participants to be realistic when planning activities but at the same time to go ahead and plan something radical if they are willing to follow through with their plans.

Objective

For people to plan a family activity and to recognize how recreation can be used to improve family relations.

Who

People who could benefit from improving family relations and who are willing to do activities with their families.

Group Size

1 or more

Materials

➲ One worksheet for each participant (found after the activity description)
➲ Pens, pencils

Description

Supply each participant with a copy of the worksheet and a pen or pencil. Allow time for individuals to fill out their worksheets. For those who finish early, offer an additional copy of the second page to fill out for additional activities that they would like to do with their families.

Once everyone has completed the worksheets, gather the group together so that they may share the activity plans they have made with the group and discuss the reasons for the answers given to the questions on the worksheets.

Discussion Topics

1. How does our family affect our lives?
2. What kind of relationship do you have with your family?
3. Do you get along better with some of your family members than you do with others?
4. Are you willing to try to make your relationship better?
5. What needs to change in you to improve family relations?

Family Activity Worksheet 1

List the activities you enjoy doing with your family now.

List the activities you would like to do with your family.

Family Activity Worksheet 2

Select one of the activities that you would like to do with your family and answer the following questions.

Name of Activity _____

1. Why doesn't your family do this now?

2. What supplies are needed for this activity?

3. What does the activity cost?

4. When would the activity take place?

5. Why did you pick this activity?

6. What would keep your family from doing this activity?

7. How could it benefit you and your family to do activities together?

SPRING BREAK PLAN

Spring break, Christmas break, Thanksgiving and all the other holidays that occur throughout the year open a door of opportunity for us to engage in positive activities or negative activities. If members of the group normally choose to spend their vacation time doing negative activities, a pre-planned vacation of healthy alternatives may be the key to helping them make better choices during the holidays.

Spring break seems to be especially geared towards unhealthy activities so people may need a plan of action more than for other, more family-oriented vacations.

Objective

For people to come up with a positive activity plan and show the ability to follow through with the plan.

Who

People who spend vacation time engaging in unhealthy leisure activities. People who do not have any idea what they will do during vacation.

Group Size

1 or more

Materials

➲ Copies of "Spring Break worksheet" found on the second following page
➲ Pens, pencils

Description

Give each person a copy of the Spring Break worksheet. Allow time for each participant to fill it out completely. Some people may wish to fill out more than one if they have more than one activity they would like to pursue during Spring Break.

Once everyone has completed their worksheet, give each person a chance to share the plan that they have created. Encourage the group to give feedback, ask questions and to decide if the plan is negative, positive and if it is realistic. If the group will be together after the break, a follow up group may be planned to discuss how the break went for everyone and whether or not they followed through with their plans.

Discussion Topics

Before the vacation:
1. Do you think your plan is realistic?
2. How difficult will it be to follow your plan?
3. What will be your biggest challenges?

After the vacation:
1. Did you follow your plan?
2. What parts were easy? What parts were hard?
3. How would you change your plan for your next vacation?

Variations

➲ This may be done for a weekend or any other vacation time that occurs.

Spring Break Worksheet

1. Will you be working during the break?

2. How much free time do you expect to have during your break?

3. What leisure activity do you plan to spend most of your time doing?

4. What supplies will be needed for this activity?

5. How much money will be needed?

6. Who else will be involved in this activity with you?

7. Do you feel this activity will be a positive or a negative experience for you, and why?

FAMILY FUN MAP

People usually relate to each member of their family differently. Some relationships are strong while others are weak or in need of repair. Relationships where communication is difficult often benefit from some recreation time where the people can get together in an activity that they both enjoy.

In this activity we will be looking for a possible activity with each family member and naming the ways it can enhance each relationship. Hopefully, this will begin the process of repairing damaged relationships and building bonds that can last a lifetime.

Objective

For people to recognize activities that can help them improve relations with family members.

Who

People who could benefit from improved relations with family members.

Group Size

1 or more

Materials

➔ Paper or copies of "Family Fun Map" (found on following page)
➔ Pens, pencils

Description

Give each participant a copy of the "Family Fun Map" or provide them with a piece of paper and instruct them to put the appropriate topics at the top of each column (see following page for example). Allow time for each person to fill out the sheet.

When everyone is finished, gather the group together and allow time for everyone to share their "Family Fun Map" with the rest of the group.

Discussion Topics

1. Do you have a poor relationship with anyone in your family? If so, who? If not, why do you feel that you have a good relationship with everyone?

2. Do you do many activities with family members that you have a poor relationship with?

3. Do you do many activities with family members that you have a good relationship with?

4. Are the new activities that you would like to do realistic for your family to do? If not, why? If so, would you be willing to pursue them, and what will you have to do?

5. Do you feel that recreation can improve your relationships? Why or why not?

Family Fun Map

Family Member	Things You Do Together Now	Things You Would Like To Do Together	How This Can Help Your Relationship

ACTIVITY ALPHABET

There are a wide range of recreational activities for anyone who has enough initiative to find them. Making people aware of some of the recreation possibilities available to them is important when you want to show them they can change their current leisure habits. Creating a large list of activities is a simple way to create awareness of the wide range of recreational activities that exist.

Once you have a list, you can start to turn it into a resource book of recreational activities and ideas. For some of the group it may be a way to get new ideas. For others it may spark an interest in things that they have forgotten that they enjoyed. By gathering activity ideas into a small book, members of the group may find ideas for things that they really want to do.

Objective

To explore and create a record of many activities that people can participate in during their free time.

Who

People who are unaware of potential recreational activities that are available to them.

Group Size

2 or more

Materials

- ➲ Paper
- ➲ Pens, pencils
- ➲ Colored markers

Description

Divide the group into two or more teams. Give each team a piece of paper that has the alphabet written down the left hand side. Have each team write down as many activities as they can think of that begin with each letter of the alphabet within a given time.

Once the time limit is up, bring the teams back together and have each team read their list to the group. Combine all of the lists to create one larger list to look at during discussion time.

Have people select activities that they like from the list and draw pictures of them. Share the pictures with each other and put them into a book to use for recreation ideas.

Discussion Topics

1. Are you surprised by how many activities the group was able to come up with?
2. Do you do many of these activities now? Why or why not?
3. Is there anything on the list that you would like to do but have never done before?
4. Is it possible for you to pursue any of these new activities?
5. What can you do if you are interested in participating in a new activity?
6. How would it benefit you to participate in a new activity?
7. What do you think the group should do with the completed book?

Variations

- Add some competition by giving teams points for each activity that they have on their lists that are not on the other team's lists.
- Give a set amount of time for each letter of the alphabet.
- This activity can be split across two or more activity times, especially if the group wants to draw many of the activities they listed.
- Make a book that you keep for different groups and let each new group add to the already existing book.

LEiSURE INTERVIEW

Some people have good leisure habits while others have bad leisure habits. Making people aware of their current behaviors and habits about how they spend their free time is the first step in making them aware of the need for change in their current leisure lifestyle.

Objective

For people to learn more about their own leisure interest and to gain ideas of new activities they may enjoy. To learn about the leisure interests of the other group members.

Who

People who could benefit from understanding their current leisure habits.

Group Size

4 or more

Materials

➲ Copies of the interview sheet (found on the following page)
➲ Pens, pencils

Description

Divide the group into pairs and give each set of partners two copies of the interview sheet and a pen or pencil. Allow time for each person to ask his/her partner the questions and to write down the answers on the interview sheet.

Once everyone is finished, gather the group together and ask the participants to tell the rest of the group about their partners' leisure interests. After each person is introduced, the group may give suggestions for new activities that they feel that person might enjoy.

Discussion Topics

Discuss the current and possible interests of each group member.

Leisure Interview

1. What do you spend most of your free time doing?

2. What benefits do you get from doing these activities?

3. Do you think that this is a good way to spend your free time?

4. What would you like to do for fun but have never done before?

5. Why haven't you done this?

6. Would you rather do activities alone or with other people? Why?

7. Do you prefer to do active things or passive things?

8. What would you like to do to improve how you spend your free time?

To be filled out when introducing your partner
9. Suggestions from the group...

TEACH AND LEARN

Learning about new activities gives people the opportunity to expand what they do during their free time. People around us know how to play many games that we don't know how to play because we have never been taught. Giving people the opportunity to teach each other games that they know how to play can open new interests and provide a new list of activities for those involved.

Objective

For people to learn new activities that can be done during free time. To discuss and explore the benefits of learning a new game or activity.

Who

People who need to change their current leisure lifestyle by adding more possible choices of activities.

Group Size

4 or more

Materials

➲ Decks of playing cards

Description

Teach the group a card game that you know and allow the group to play at least one hand of the game. After teaching the game, ask for a different volunteers to teach any new card game to the group. Allow time to play each new game for at least one hand.

Give as many people a chance to teach a new game as time allows or until people run out of new ideas, at which time you may wish to spend more time playing one of the new games learned.

Discussion Topics

1. Did you learn any new games today that you had never played before?
2. Do you ever feel bored at home and feel that you want to do something new?
3. What are some ways to learn a new activity?
4. What benefit would it be for you to learn new activities?

Variations

➲ This is a great activity to do in a gymnasium to allow kids to teach new active games to the group and then to play the new games.

ONE MiNUTE

There are many benefits that you can get from participating in recreational activities. Identifying what the benefits are and recognizing the value found in a particular activity are important when considering what type of activities are best for each person in the group. Many people often do not stop to think of the benefits that they can get out of a recreational activity until they are asked, as they are in the course of this simple game.

Objective

To promote discussion of the benefits of participating in leisure activities.

Who

People who are unaware of the benefits that they can get out of participating in a recreational activity.

Group Size

4 or more

Materials

➲ Paper
➲ Pens, pencils
➲ Copies of questions (found on following two pages)

Description

Divide the group into two teams and send one team out of the room. The team remaining in the room is given one minute to answer as many of the six questions as they can from one of the sets of questions. Assign one team member the job of writing down the answers for each question or simply record the number of appropriate answers given. Read one question every ten seconds and record the answers given in that time period.

Once the minute is up, bring the other team back into the room and do the same for them, but do not let them see the answers given by the other team. Tally up all the answers at the end of each round to determine the score. Continue in this manner until you complete all four rounds.

Discussion Topics

1. How easy was it to think of reasons for doing activities?
2. Do you ever think about why you do the activities that you do?
3. Name your favorite activity and the benefits that you get from participating in that activity.

Variations

➲ If you have two leaders, you can get the answers from both groups at the same time.
➲ Think up more questions about leisure activities for additional rounds.
➲ Use this format to do the ALPHABET RACE.

One Minute Question Sheet

Round 1
1. Games that start with the letter C?

2. Activities to do with friends?

3. School events?

4. Reasons that people go to football games?

5. Activities to help you relax?

6. What you've learned from being with this group?

Round 2
1. Winter activities?

2. Activities to do alone?

3. Games that start with the letter S?

4. Activities that can release anger?

5. Places that kids hang out in the summer?

6. Reasons people go bowling?

THE WRECKING YARD

Round 3

1. Winter Olympic events?

2. Activities to do with a family?

3. Summer activities?

4. Reasons people play video games?

5. Things to do to meet other people?

6. Popular movies?

Round 4

1. Places to go for Spring Break?

2. Sports that help people learn self-discipline?

3. Reasons that people watch TV?

4. Favorite places to go swimming?

5. Things to do during summer vacation?

6. Games that this group has played together?

INTEREST SPARKER

Talking about getting involved in new activities is one thing, but trying new things out to become aware of new interests and activities is another. If people are exposed to a wide variety of games and activities, they will probably find something that they are interested in pursuing that they would not have tried on their own. This activity gives group members a chance to find new ideas that are interesting for them.

Objective

To increase awareness of new activities that people may eventually pursue on their own.

Who

People who need to add more variety to their current leisure lifestyle.

Group Size

Varies

Materials

➲ Varies

Description

Provide a new activity or game for the group to spark interest in that activity and to promote discussion of ways that the new activity may be pursued once group members are no longer with the group.

Interest Sparker ideas...
➲ Any arts and crafts projects
➲ Singing, playing musical instruments
➲ Drama, skits
➲ A variety of sports activities
➲ Any hobbies (i.e. sewing, building models, cooking)
➲ Poetry, writing letters, stories

⊃ Reading (visit library)

Discussion Topics

1. Was this a new activity for you? If so, would you be interested in becoming more involved in it?
2. How can you find ways to become involved in this activity in your community?
3. How do you feel you could benefit from becoming involved in this activity?
4. Is there something you would like to try but have never done before? If so, what and why haven't you?
5. What steps can you take to become more involved in any new activity?

BORED BOARD

People have a hard time understanding that being bored requires them to take action — that their boredom is not someone else's problem. Being bored means they need to take another step, to change what they are doing.

At the same time, people who are bored a lot tend to have a poor understanding that they have the opportunity to choose between good and bad leisure options, if they realize that they have any options at all. Being "bored" is being on the threshold of potential ruin or happiness. This activity is to help group members find out that they have choices and to list some of the choices that are good for them.

Objective

For people to understand what it means to be bored. To explore ways of dealing with being bored and to find appropriate activities to do during leisure time.

Who

People who can't think of good activities for their leisure time.

Group Size

1 or more

Materials

- A thin board for each person in the group (about 2 x 8 in)
- Marking pens
- One question sheet for each person (found on the second following page)

Description

Start the group by having each person fill out a question sheet and then discuss the answers as a group. After the discussion, hand out blank boards and instruct the group to write down as many free time activities as they can think of.

Once everyone has completed this task, allow group members to share what they have written on their board so that others in the group may write down the ideas that they like for their own boards. Encourage group members to keep their boards and to look at them when they are bored and to do one of the activities that they have written down.

Discussion Topics

Discuss worksheet and explore whether group members ever feel
depressed when bored or if they act out and get into trouble. Emphasize
the importance of finding activities to do that are easily accessible, safe
and appropriate.

Bored Board Questions

1. What does it mean to be bored?

2. What do you do when you are bored?

3. What do you feel like when you are bored?

4. Do you ever do anything that is dangerous to yourself or to someone else when you are bored? If so what?

5. Name some positive activities that you do to relieve your boredom.

COMMUNICATION SKILLS

Communication is the act of transferring information from one person to another. The information may be facts but, even more important, is the effective communication of feelings or emotions.

A child who has difficulty following directions, a teenage boy who can't talk to his dad about his feelings of inadequacy, a teenage girl who throws bricks through the window of her parents' home when she is angry rather than expressing her feelings verbally — these are just a few examples of youth I have worked with who need better communication skills. Learning how to listen to others better, share feelings and discuss problems is a key part of growing up.

Games and activities can become useful tools for teaching communication skills. Every game has rules and directions that must be communicated and followed for the game to go smoothly. Teamwork requires good verbal and listening skills for the team to be successful. If there is ever a dispute during the game, it may be worked out by talking it out. There are many aspects of communication during every game that we play.

In other chapters of this book there are many games that focus on topics besides communication skills, but in all of them there is an underlying need for clear communication. This chapter is filled with games that focus specifically on the need for clear communication skills and stresses the importance of paying attention to communication from others. Much of our communication is verbal, so that is what is emphasized in this chapter, but non-verbal communication is important, too, as you will see in SiLENT VOLLEYBALL and other activities.

COMMUNICATION SKILLS ACTIVITIES

SILENT VOLLEYBALL (WITH A TWIST)

We often take for granted our ability to communicate our wants and needs to others by speaking. When our ability to speak is taken away (such as in a foreign country), we must find other ways to get our needs met.

Gestures, body language or drawing pictures are all examples of ways we can communicate nonverbally. These alternative methods of communication are an important part of conveying any message, whether we can speak or not.

Objective

To increase understanding of the importance of being able to communicate clearly with others.

Who

People who have a difficult time communicating clearly to others.

Group Size

4 to 12 participants

Materials

- Envelopes
- One marking pen
- Pieces of wrapped candy
- Volleyball
- Volleyball net

Description

Give each person in the group an envelope filled with five pieces of candy. Ask each person to write his/her name on the outside of the envelope. Place all of the envelopes beside the court so that all of the names are visible to the group.

State the following rules to the group prior to playing volleyball:

1. Play volleyball by the regular volleyball rules.
2. At no time during the game may anyone talk.
3. If someone is caught talking, the first person in the group who calls out that person's name may take one piece of candy out of the envelope of the person who talked and place it in his/her own envelope. Calling out a name is the only talking that is allowed during the game.
4. The leader will determine if someone did indeed talk and determine who called out the name first.

Once the game is over, the leader will announce that talking is allowed. Everyone may then go and get their candy and eat it during discussion time.

Discussion Topics

1. Was it difficult not to talk? Why or why not?
2. What would have been different about your team if talking had been allowed?
3. When working with a team, why is communication important?
4. If you became frustrated at any time during the game, how did you cope with your frustration?

Variations

➲ Volleyball isn't the only game that may be used for this activity. Candy envelopes work well for many different games.
➲ If you are health conscious or choose not to use candy, peanuts in the shells are a great alternative.

FOLLOW DIRECTIONS OBSTACLE COURSE

People seem to have an uncanny ability to follow directions during a fun game, when they benefit from following the directions or any other time they think they will gain something. At other times they seem to develop a sudden inability to hear you or have difficulty understanding what is going on. Funny how it works, isn't it?

By making it clear to people that you recognize they are choosing when to follow and when not to follow directions, you are able to give them the message that you know what their true abilities are.

Objective

For people to recognize the difference between having the ability to follow directions and making the choice to follow directions.

Who

People who have difficulty following directions.

Group Size

4 to 10 participants

Materials

- Copy of direction sheet (found on the following page)
- Paper bag

Description

Copy the sheet of directions and cut it into slips of paper so that one direction is on each piece of paper. Place the directions into a paper bag. Spread the group out in the play area with enough room to run around.

Once everyone is in a designated spot, pass the bag around for everyone to pick out a direction and to read it to him/herself. Choose one group member to go through the direction obstacle course first. S/he runs from person to person. Each time the runner comes to a person, that person must read the direction on his/her slip of paper. The runner must complete the direction and then go to the next person to receive the next direction and so on, until s/he has received a direction from each member of the group.

Emphasize the importance of reading the directions clearly and that each direction should only be read once. Place the directions back into the bag after each person has completed the course and have each group member draw out a new direction before the next person goes through the course.

Discussion Topics

1. Was it easy for you to follow all of the directions? Why or why not?
2. Do you ever have difficulty following directions? If so, why?
3. Do you ever choose not to follow directions? Why or why not?
4. Why is it important to be able to follow directions given to you?

Variations

➲ Create a different list of directions.
➲ Time how long it takes for people to go through the course and then give them the chance to go through it again in attempt to beat their previous time.

Follow Direction Obstacle Course

1. Give everyone a "high five."
2. Touch each wall in the room.
3. Say the entire alphabet.
4. Sing "Row, row, row, your boat" three times.
5. Do ten jumping jacks.
6. Pat your head and rub your tummy three times.
7. Run around in a circle five times.
8. Shake hands with four different people.
9. Do three sit ups.
10. Name three things that you are good at doing.

BLIND MAP WALK

Giving and receiving directions over the phone is much more difficult than giving them in person. When you are talking on the phone, you need clear communication skills for both parties to understand each other. In this game success depends on clear verbal skills and excellent listening skills.

Objective

For people to learn the importance of giving clear directions and to learn what is required of them when using good listening skills. To build trust among group members.

Who

People who could benefit from learning how to communicate more clearly and listen to others better.

Group Size

2 or more (an even number is best)

Materials

➲ Blindfolds
➲ A sketch of the surrounding area with a course drawn on it

Description

Divide the group into pairs and blindfold one member of each pair. Give the partner, without the blindfold, a copy of the map. The partner without the blindfold must guide the blindfolded partner through the course with only verbal directions. The partners may walk together but they may not touch each other.

Once the course has been completed, switch the blindfold to the other partner and give the pair a new map to follow.

HINT: This works best when you use an area that is unfamiliar to the group so they do not already know what obstacles they may encounter.

Discussion Topics

1. Did you like giving or receiving directions the best? Why?
2. What did you do to make sure the directions were clearly understood?
3. What did you do to make sure you were following the directions?
4. Why are good communication skills important?
5. How was trust a factor in this activity?

DiRECTiON DiRECTiON

In our society there is a constant transfer of information from one person to another. You must be careful when you pass information on if you want it to stay accurate. One great example shows up in rules for a game. If you check with people in different parts of the country, you will find out that many of the games have different rules. Someone, sometime changed the rules a little bit.

In this activity someone gets a set of rules and the group gets to see how easy it can be to make mistakes in passing them on. This can be a fun way to see what can happen when information is not passed on correctly.

Objective

For people to recognize the importance of using good communication skills when giving directions and when receiving directions. To recognize the difficulties encountered when interpreting what someone else said.

Who

People who believe everything they hear.
People who could benefit from listening carefully to directions and passing them along correctly.

Group Size

2 or more

Materials

➲ Varies

Description

Chose a game that a has a few specific rules that must be followed in order to play the game (and enough rules to make it hard to remember them all). Prior to the activity select one person and give him/her the directions for the game without telling the rest of the group. Verbally explain the game and clearly state all of the rules.

At the time of the game, the person who has heard the rules will give the directions to the rest of the group without any help from you. Allow the group to play the game at least once through before having a group discussion or making any corrections or clarifications in the rules of the game.

Discussion Topics

1. Was there any confusion about the rules of the game?
2. Why do you think the game was explained correctly (or incorrectly)?
3. What is important to remember when listening to others and when giving directions?

Variations

➲ Select a game that requires two teams. Separate the two teams and select one member from each team to receive the directions for the game. Each person explains the rules to his/her team.
➲ Give each team a different set of directions, on purpose.

BACK TO BACK

Instruction manuals must be clearly written for people who read them to follow the directions correctly. For many tasks it is so much easier to just show someone how to do it. This activity doesn't let you do it the easy way.

Explaining without showing is a lot like writing an instruction manual. You need to consider many different possible ways to make mistakes when you tell someone what to do. You need to find ways to make the task clear and simple to follow. This activity will show the group just how hard giving good directions can be.

Objective

For people to understand the importance of giving clear, concise directions.

Who

People who need to work on precision and detail in their communication skills.

Group Size

2 or more

Materials

➲ Paper
➲ Pens, pencils

Description

Divide the group into pairs. Give each person two pieces of paper and a pen or pencil. Instruct each set of partners to sit back to back, so that neither partner can see the other person's paper. Each person draws a simple picture on his/her paper.

The partners then take turns describing their pictures to each other (without stating what the picture is if it is a known object) in an attempt to get their partner to accurately draw what is described. Once both the drawings are completed, ask the partners to share their pictures with each other and compare how similar or different they are.

Discussion Topics

1. How do you feel you and your partner did at this activity?
2. What was difficult about this activity?
3. What aspect of communication is most difficult for you?
4. Is it easier for you to explain things or to listen to others? Why?
5. What did your partner do to make this activity easier for you?
6. When is it important to have clear communication skills?

Variations

➲ The activity may be done with one person explaining a hidden picture to the rest of the group.
➲ Make stipulations on the activity (i.e. questions are not allowed to be asked, yes/no questions may be asked, any questions may be asked when the directions are given).
➲ Do the activity a number of times with a different stipulation for each round and compare the differences at the end.
➲ May use popcicle sticks, clay, dominos, etc. to build a simple sculpture that must be described.

TACTILE TELEPHONE

We can only hope that others receive accurate information about us when "gossip" is taking place. If the information being passed along is not carefully transferred from one individual to another, the end result may be the same as it usually is at the end of this simple game.

Objective

To observe how messages can get altered as they are passed along.

Who

People who could benefit from learning about how little information is passed along accurately.

Group Size

3 or more

Materials

➲ Paper
➲ Pens, pencils

Description

Prior to the activity make an assortment of simple line drawings. Gather the group together, instructing them to sit on the floor, single file, facing the back of the person sitting in front of them. The last person is given one of the drawings and the first person is given a piece of paper and a pen or pencil.

The last person in line looks at the picture and draws it on the back of the person in front of him/her, using only his/her finger. Every person in the line tries to copy what they felt on their back to the back of the person in front of them. When the first person in line receives the drawing, s/he draws it on the paper. Compare the original drawing to the drawing at the end and see how close the group came to passing the drawing on accurately.

Discussion Topics

1. How do you feel the group did at this activity?
2. Did the picture change as it traveled? Why or why not?
3. Do you always believe everything you hear? Why or why not?
4. Do you ever notice information being changed as it is passed along?
5. What is important to remember when you are having a conversation with someone else?

Variations

➲ Have each person draw what they felt on a piece of paper after they pass it on to see how the drawing changed as it moved along the line.

20 STEP DIRECTIONS

Some information is easy to remember and other information is not. Being able to listen to directions and remember what has been said is an important skill to learn. This activity will show you how well the group can follow instructions.

Objective

To show the importance of listening to directions carefully.

Who

People who need to learn how to listen to directions.

Group Size

1 or more

Materials

➲ A list of 20 different directions (see following page)

Description

Come up with a list of twenty different instructions that can easily be done one at a time (a list of ideas follows). Instruct participants to sit down once they have followed the directions given to them and tell them that no one may begin until the direction has been completely read.

Read the first direction for the group to follow. Once the direction is completely read, everyone must follow it as closely as they can. Then repeat the first direction again and add the second. Continue in this pattern, adding one more direction each time, until all twenty directions have been read. Remind them, if you need to, to sit down after they have completed the current set of directions.

Discussion Topics

1. Were you able to follow all the directions? If so, what helped you to remember all of the directions?
2. Is it difficult or easy for you to listen to others and follow directions?
3. If it is difficult for you to follow directions, what can you do to improve your listening skills?
4. Why is it important to be able to follow directions?

20 Step Directions

1. Stand up
2. Turn around
3. Clap your hands
4. Touch the wall
5. Shake someone's hand
6. Do a jumping jack
7. Hop on one foot
8. Give someone a hug
9. Say the alphabet
10. Do one push up
11. Give someone a "high five"
12. Shout your name
13. Jump up in the air
14. Touch your toes
15. Smile
16. Count to 10
17. Do a sit up
18. Stomp your feet
19. Sing "row, row, row your boat"
20. Shout "HOORAY!"

PICTURE NOT SO PERFECT

Using descriptive language is a good way to improve basic communication skills and enhance your vocabulary. Imagine trying to tell someone to draw a picture of an elephant without being able to use the word elephant.

In this activity the group members get a chance to see how they might solve that problem. This is a chance for the group to enhance its verbal and listening skills by describing a picture without being able to say what the picture really is. It's a challenge.

Objective

To enhance verbal communication skills and to stress the importance of paying close attention to others when they are talking.

Who

People who need to improve their ability to use language.

Group Size

2 or more

Materials

➲ Paper
➲ Colored markers
➲ Copies of picture instructions (found on following pages)

Description

Provide paper and colored markers for everyone in the group. Select one person to give the directions of what is to be drawn. The person giving the instructions must imagine the details of a picture based on the description given. Then s/he describes the picture s/he imagined without using any of the words listed below the description. The rest of the group attempts to draw a picture matching what the describer tells them to draw, based on what they hear. Allow time for the group members to view each other's pictures, after each description is completed.

Discussion Topics

1. If you were one of the people selected to give directions, how did you feel when you were describing your picture to the group?
2. What was important for you to do when listening to the description?
3. What do you do when you encounter someone who doesn't give clear directions? What should you do?

Variations

➲ Give one set of descriptions to everyone in the group and have them draw their own picture first, before describing it to the rest of the group.

Picture Not So Perfect Instructions

Picture 1
A waterfall flowing between two mountains and a rainbow connecting the two mountains, with a bright sun in the sky.

Don't use the words:

Waterfall

Mountain

Colors

Rainbow

Sun

Picture 2
An island in the middle of the ocean with two palm trees on it, with coconuts under the trees and a sailboat in the water in the distance.

Don't use the words:

Island

Sailboat

Coconut

Ocean

Palm tree

Picture 3
An airplane in the sky that is flying in front of a football stadium, pulling a banner that says "Happy Birthday Joe".

Don't use the words:

Airplane

Stadium

Happy Birthday

Football

Banner

Picture 4

A person in a green baseball hat waiting at a bus stop. There is a stop sign in the background and a garbage can under the stop sign.

Don't use the words:

Bus	Stop
Garbage	Green
Hat	

Picture 5

A dog is at the bottom of a tree barking at a cat that is stuck in the tree. The tree is in front of house with a bike sitting in the driveway.

Don't use the words:

Dog	Cat
Tree	House
Bike	

Picture 6

A desert with two large cacti in it and a drinking fountain between the two cacti. A bird is sitting on the fountain and there are three clouds in the sky.

Don't use the words:

Desert	Cactus
Bird	Fountain
Clouds	

CHANGE CHALLENGE

Allowing people to lead and follow the lead of others gives them the opportunity to practice giving clear directions to others and to listen carefully to what others have to say.

Objective

For people to improve listening skills and to understand the importance of having good listening skills. To enhance verbal skills for participants when they give directions to the group.

Who

People who have difficulty listening to and following directions.

Group Size

4 or more

Materials

➲ A variety of game equipment that can be found in the facility (i.e. balls, jump ropes, scooters, Frisbees™, etc.)

Description

Based upon the equipment available, create a simple relay race. Explain the relay race only once to the group and them let them attempt to follow the directions given. After the first relay race, select a volunteer to create a different relay race, Allow him/her to give the directions only once so the group must listen carefully. Give as many people a chance to create a relay race as time allows.

Discussion Topics

1. Was it difficult to have the directions given to you only once? Why?
2. Is it difficult to give directions only once? Why?
3. Was there ever any frustration during this activity? If so, why?
4. Is there ever a time when you get to hear instructions only once? When?
5. Why is it important to be able to speak clearly?
6. Why is it important to be able to understand directions clearly?

ARE YOU LISTENING

During any conversation there are many different types of communication going on at the same time, some are obvious and some are not. Recognizing all the different types of communication that take place during group interaction is interesting and helps people to become more aware of all the factors involved in the process of communication.

Objective

For people to recognize skills needed in order to communicate clearly to others.

Who

People who could benefit from improving their communication skills.

Group Size

3 to 12 participants

Materials

- ➲ Paper
- ➲ Pens, pencils
- ➲ Various game supplies

Description

Prior to the activity, write the following headings on separate pieces of paper:
1. Examples of good listening skills.
2. Examples of poor listening skills.
3. Examples of anyone using body language to communicate with others.
4. Examples of anyone using clear verbal skills.
5. Examples of anyone using poor verbal skills.
6. Examples of anyone using their tone of voice as a way to communicate feelings.

Set up a game or an activity that is interactive but has directions that must be followed (i.e. board games, cards, croquet, etc.).

At the beginning of the game, pass out the papers with the headings on them to the different group members. If there are more than six people in the group, give the same heading to more than one person. Tell everyone to keep their heading a secret. Throughout the game each person should observe the interactions of the group and write down any observations that correspond with the heading on the top of his/her paper.

Once the game is over, gather the group together and allow each person to read his/her observations to the rest of the group.

Discussion Topics

1. Are you surprised by what everyone observed during the game?
2. Do you have anything to add to any of the lists?
3. Why is it important to be aware of what are good and what are poor communication skills?
4. What should you do to show good listening skills?
5. What should you do to show good verbalization skills?

MISSING WORDS

Leading a group in a new game is sometimes difficult. The directions and rules must be conveyed clearly so everyone understands the new game correctly. If you are learning a new game, your job is to listen carefully to the directions so you can play the game the way it is supposed to be played. Sometimes simple games may not be so simple to explain or understand in the beginning unless those involved use good communication and listening skills.

Objective

For people to enhance their verbal communication skills. To stress the importance of paying close attention to others when they are talking.

Who

People who need to practice expressing themselves and people who need to practice listening carefully.

Group Size

2 or more

Materials

- A copy of the MISSING WORDS directions, found on the following pages.
- Volleyball net
- Volleyball
- Hula hoop
- Jump rope
- Basketball
- Basketball hoop
- Foosball table
- Foosball

Description

Gather the group together and select a volunteer to give the first set of directions to the group. The rest of the group must pay close attention to the directions that are given and attempt to do what they are told to do.

Continue with the other sets of directions with each leader following the special instructions for his/her set of directions (see MiSSiNG WORDS directions found on the following pages).

Discussion Topics

1. Which set of directions was most difficult for you to follow? Why?
2. When is it most difficult for you to follow directions?
3. Why is it important to be able to follow directions?
4. Do you feel people usually understand what you say?

Variations

➔ Make up your own MiSSiNG WORDS directions, based on the equipment that is available in your facility.

Missing Words Directions

Direction 1

You must give the group the instructions without using your voice. You can use gestures but you may not actually do the thing you are telling the group to do. You may answer "yes" or "no" to questions that anyone ask you.

Instruct the group set up the volleyball net, hit the ball over the net a few times and take the net down before sitting on the floor in a circle.

Direction 2

You must verbally give the following instructions to the group, but you may not use any of the words listed below.

Instruct the group to hula hoop five times each, then jump rope ten times each before sitting back down on the floor.

Hula hoop
Five
Jump rope
Ten
Turn
Sit

Direction 3

With your back to the group, give the group the following instructions.

Instruct the group to each pick up a basketball and to make one basket into the hoop. When they are done, they should sit down against the wall.

Direction 4

You must give the group the instructions without using your voice and the group may not ask you any questions.

Instruct the group to play one game of foosball as teams (each person controlling one handle) to a score of five. All the tallest people should be on one team and all the shortest people on the other team.

Direction 5

You must give the group the following instructions and you may not repeat any of the instructions, answer any of the questions or let the group know that they will only receive the instructions once.

Instruct the group to wait until all of the instructions are given before they can begin. Each person in the group must give everyone else in the group a "high five", then touch the wall, join hands to form a circle, circle around four times, drop hands, run in place for ten seconds and then sit down in a circle.

ANGER MANAGEMENT

An eleven year old boy was talking about his anger control problem with one of the therapists on the inpatient psychiatric unit where I was working. In his short life, this boy has an extensive history of violence and of becoming excessively aggressive when angered. He had asked to talk with the therapist because he was looking for answers on ways to control his anger. During the conversation he talked about how he was made fun of at school and how he "exploded" when this happened. He knew that he was in the psychiatric hospital in order to get help and was concerned that, if he didn't show his anger while in the hospital, he would not get help. He suggested that the hospital staff and the other patients make fun of him so that he could practice using anger control skills within the safe environment of the hospital with the therapist there to help him if he needed it. Some people may think that this is a crazy idea, but if we step back and think about it, this may not be as crazy as it seems.

Recently I took a class on how to telemark ski. Although I had been cross county skiing since I was four years old, I hadn't been able to master the difficult task of making turns on a steep slope when going down a hill (a telemark turn). During the class we met in a classroom and learned about all the aspects of skiing in the back country, such as avalanche safety, equipment and ski gear. Then we brought our skis into the classroom and practiced the technical skills needed for making a telemark turn with our skis on the flat carpet. Had the class stopped at this point, I would have learned some good tips but my skiing wouldn't have improved dramatically. Improvement did not occur until we went up into the mountains for some skiing sessions with our instructor. As we skidded down the slopes on our faces and finally recovered, our instructor gave us many pointers, instructions, reminders and demonstrations. By the end of the first skiing session, all I had learned in the classroom was beginning to make sense and, after a few more sessions, I became proficient at making telemark turns on even the steepest of slopes. Just as we wouldn't expect someone to learn how to ski without the instructor guiding them through the process, we shouldn't expect people to learn anger control by simply sitting in a classroom, listening to an instructor or by reading a book.

It is important to learn the basics of any skill before attempting to use it but, once the basics are learned, practice is required for mastery. Recreation is such a powerful way to teach anger control because competition, rivalry and frustration often occur in a competitive game and may spark anger in those who are easily angered. Becoming angry during a game is like falling down on the easy slope when skiing. It doesn't hurt as much when you fall on the easy slope and others are around to help you get up and move on down the hill. Likewise, anger that is sparked during a simple game isn't usually as intense as anger triggered in more volatile situations.

When an individual does become angry during a game, there is support from peers and staff as to how to deal with the anger. The game needs to be stopped when an individual needs support from others in order to control his/her anger or when the group or an individual needs to talk about what is going on. If the game goes smoothly and nobody in the group displays any anger, focus the discussion on the success of the activity and the use of good anger control skills that were displayed during the game.

Recreation activities are not only good for giving youth the opportunity to practice anger management but also offer a way for people to appropriately release their anger. Helping youth to discover ways to release anger and to find new activities that they can pursue, as a means of anger management, is an important role that recreation can play in teaching anger control.

ANGER MANAGEMENT ACTIVITIES

ANGER AWARENESS

Everyone gets angry. Most people make poorer choices when they are angry. Sometimes people make choices that are so bad they wonder how they ever could have been so stupid. Most people solve the problem by not making choices or doing anything significant when they are angry. They cool down first and then decide what to do.

What if someone can't tell when they are angry? How can they know when to stop doing things and wait to calm down? Often, if we pay attention, our body will tell us that we are angry before our mind catches on. This activity will help the group members find some of the things their bodies do when they are angry. Then in other activities, they can look for the clues and have a better chance of controlling their anger before it gets out of control.

Objective

For the group to explore the physical responses that go along with anger and to identify appropriate ways to deal with these responses.

Who

People who have trouble knowing when they are angry.

Group Size

2 or more

Materials

- ➲ Large poster size pieces of paper
- ➲ Sheets of drawing paper
- ➲ Markers
- ➲ Glue

Description

Ask the group to think about what happens to their bodies when they get angry. Make a list on one of the sheets of poster paper of all of the physical feelings that the group members associate with the feeling of anger.

Once the list is completed, look over the list as a group and then make another list containing appropriate ways to release these angry feelings. Once both of the lists are completed, allow each group member to select one of the appropriate ways of dealing with anger and draw a picture of it. Once everyone has finished drawing a picture, glue all of the pictures onto the poster size paper to create a wall hanging of "anger alternatives" to display where the group meets regularly.

Discussion Topics

1. Why is it so hard to figure out when you are angry?
2. Which of these cues will help you the most? Why?
3. How do you normally release your anger? Do you feel that this is a good way to release anger? Why or why not?
4. How many things on the list would you be willing to do to release your anger?
5. Why is it important to find appropriate ways to release anger?

ANGER RELEASE

Feeling angry is normal. Everyone feels angry some time. The question is what to do when you feel angry. Some people release their anger appropriately and some do not. Hurting yourself or another person or something of value is not something that you can do. If members of the group have this problem, they need to explore other alternatives.

One goal of this activity is for group members to think of something that makes them feel really angry. The second goal is to find a way to get through the anger in an acceptable way. There are always choices for dealing with feelings. This activity will help the explore some of the possible alternatives.

Objective

To explore alternative ways to release anger that do not harm one's self, others or property.

Who

People who express their anger inappropriately.

Group Size

1 or more

Materials

Any of the following...
- Exercise equipment
- Blown up balloons (to be popped)
- Soccer ball, basketball, football, etc.
- An area to run in
- Plastic tipped darts and dart board
- Jump rope
- A variety of different types of music accessible by headphones
- A place to scream
- Someone to talk with

- Paper and pen or pencil
- Anything else available that can be used as an anger management tool

Description

Make the materials that you have chosen available so that people have a variety of anger management tools. Before you use the materials, hold a group discussion where everyone talks about and thinks about things that make them really angry. Once everyone is thinking about things that make them angry and is actually feeling angry, allow them to use the equipment as a means of releasing their anger.

Once everyone is finished, have them come back to the group for discussion time. You may wish to end this group with some relaxation time (i.e. soft music or reading to the group quietly). It is a good idea to do this activity with trained staff, in case someone has difficulty releasing his/her anger appropriately.

Discussion Topics

1. Did you manage to get really angry? As angry as you get in the rest of your life?
2. How do you usually choose to release your anger?
3. How did you feel today after releasing your anger in the way that you chose?
4. Was this a better option for you than the way that you usually release your anger?
5. What are some ways of releasing your anger that would make you feel better but at the same time would not hurt anyone or anything?
6. Will you be able to use anything you did today in your own life? Which things? If not, why not?
7. Will these methods of releasing anger work in real life or do you get so much angrier in real situations that what you did here won't be effective without more practice?

BEWARE AWARE

Anger is not a simple thing. Each of us has our own things that make us angry. We each have our own ways of feeling angry and our own ways of dealing with our anger. Something that really bothers one person may not bother their friends at all.

Controlling your anger is important if you plan to stay out of trouble. One of the most important parts of controlling your anger is to understand it. That's what this activity is about: figuring out what makes people in the group angry, figuring out how they feel when they get angry and finding ways to deal with their anger.

Objective

For people to understand the process they go through when they become angry and to explore appropriate ways of dealing with anger.

Who

People who are not aware of their anger and have problems controlling what they do when they are angry.

Group Size

2 to 24 participants

Materials

- four poster-size sheets of paper
- four fat-tipped, colored markers

Description

Place one of the sheets of paper and one of the fat-tipped markers in four separate areas of the room. At the top of each of the pieces of paper write one of the following statements.

1. Make a list of things that make you angry.

2. Make a list of ways that your body feels physically when you are angry.
3. Make a list of ways that you have dealt with your anger.
4. Make a list of ways to release anger and gain control of yourself without hurting anyone or damaging anything.

Divide the group into four small groups and assign each group to a piece of paper. Once they are at the paper, the group must read the statement at the top and begin to work as a group to compile a list based on their topic. Once each group creates a list, bring the groups back together and have the groups read their lists to the rest of the group, starting with the first list.

Discussion Topics

1. Which list can you relate to the most? Why?
2. Is there anything that anyone thinks should be added to any of the lists?
3. What is the process that someone goes through when becoming angry?
4. What is usually the outcome when you become angry? What would you like the outcome to be?
5. What can you do to change the way that you handle your anger?
6. What do you see on the last list that you would most likely use as an appropriate way to release your anger?

SELF-CONTROL SWITCH

If we all used self-control when we got angry, there would probably be fewer fights and more chances to solve problems instead of making them worse. One of the important things to know when we are angry is that we can still make choices.

This activity is about making good choices instead of bad choices. The members of the group will see that using self-control is important when we are angry because it allows the person to make better choices than they would if they left their anger in control.

Objective

For people to understand the need for self-control when they become angry. For people to learn ways of exercising self-control when it is needed.

Who

People who have difficulty controlling their anger.

Group Size

4 or more

Materials

➲ Paper
➲ Pens, pencils

Description

Begin the activity by asking the group to answer the following question. "What does it mean to have self-control?" After a discussion of the definition of self-control, divide the group into smaller groups of two to four members each. Give each group a piece of paper and a pen or pencil. Ask each small group to make a list of five different examples of times when someone in the group did not use self-control or when a group member observed someone else (outside of the group) who did not use self-control.

Once the lists are completed, collect them all and then give each list to another group. Each group looks at the new list and, for each situation, lists an alternative way that the incident could have been handled. Allow time for sharing at the end and use the information given to move on to further discussion on the importance of using self-control when dealing with a situation where someone becomes angry.

Discussion Topics

1. What kinds of things made people angry?
2. Did the lack of self-control look like a good choice in any of the cases? Why or why not?
3. How much better were the alternative choices? Would they really solve the problems that made the person angry?
4. What are some of the things we can do in our own lives to ensure that we maintain our self-control?

ANGER CHOICE

Some people explode when they are angry while others keep things inside and let their anger eat at them. Some people get boiling hot and some people get ice cold. From one extreme to the other, it is important for group members to look at themselves and recognize how they handle their anger. This activity helps the group members become aware of the choices that they make. That understanding moves everyone a step closer to making good, healthy choices.

Objective

For people to recognize ways that they handle their anger and to open up conversation about appropriate ways to handle anger.

Who

People who don't understand their anger and how to deal with it appropriately.

Group Size

1 or more

Materials

➲ None

Description

Read the following list of choices to the group and ask participants to choose the one that they feel fits them best. Designate a place to stand for each choice (i.e. one side of the room for choice A and the other side for choice B).

After each choice is read and participants make their choices, ask them to explain why they chose what they chose. Then get the group back together and go on to the next set of choices.

When you are angry are you most like...

    A. Shaken can of pop   B. A cup of coffee

A. Lake   B. Ocean

A. Hammer   B. Nail

A. Swimmer   B. Hockey player

A. Flute   B. Trumpet

A. Steak   B. Hamburger

A. Tiger   B. Kitty cat

A. Lava   B. Avalanche

Discussion Topics

1. Why did you pick your response?
2. Do you think the other people in the group made correct choices?
3. Do you think that your choice is really the best choice?

Variations

➲ Designate four areas in the room for choices a, b, c or d. Read the situations (found below) and ask participants to choose how they would react to the situation.

Situation Choices

1. Your friend breaks your favorite pair of very expensive sunglasses. You...
   a. Say, "It's okay it was an accident."
   b. Yell at him/her and make sure s/he feels bad.
   c. Break his/her sunglasses.
   d. Make him/her pay for them.

2. Your friend is supposed to be at your house at 7:00 and doesn't show up until 8:00 and gives you no excuse. Inside you feel very upset and hurt. You...
   a. Act like it doesn't bother you and let it go.
   b. Act like you just got ready and were running late also.
   c. Tell your friend that you made other plans and would have to cancel.
   d. Ask your friend to explain why s/he is late and then express your feelings.

3. Someone that you know very well tells you that your shirt is really ugly and teases you about how much weight you have gained lately. You...
   a. Swear at him/her and make fun of him/her.
   b. Ignore him/her and walk away.
   c. Tell the person that the comment was rude, that you didn't appreciate it and that it hurt your feelings.
   d. Punch the person in the face and tell him/her to "shut up."

THE BUMP SNEAK

Some people play by the rules and some people don't. There are many ways to handle people who don't follow the rules (or perhaps have different rules). Referees certainly help but they are not always around.

It can be very frustrating to play in a game where no one is around to enforce the rules, especially when someone is cheating. This game will give the group a chance to deal with the frustration of playing a game when cheating is going on and, perhaps, even find a way to stop the cheating.

Objective

For people to show the ability to appropriately control anger and frustration when confronted with cheating during a competitive game.

Who

People who cheat or get mad when other people cheat.

Group Size

4 or more

Materials

➲ Two basketballs

Description

Prior to playing the basketball game "Bump" (directions follow) select a member of the group and, without telling anyone else, instruct him/her to play the first game by the rules but to cheat during subsequent games. The best cheat is to knock the other person's ball away so it takes him/her longer to get it and shoot again. If some of the players look to you for help, shrug your shoulders and tell them to solve the problem. If the group comes up with a good solution to the cheating, stop the game and explain that the person was cheating because you told him/her to. Tell him/her that s/he doesn't have to cheat any more and let the game go on.

Bump Instructions

Line the group up single file behind the free throw line on a basketball court, giving the first two people in line a basketball. The first person in line takes a shot at the basket from the line. If the basket is made, s/he goes to the end of the line, but if the basket is missed, s/he keeps shooting the ball from anywhere on the court until the ball goes in. The second person in line takes his/her shot at the basket as soon as the first person has shot, in an attempt to make a basket before the other person does, thus eliminating that person.

Once a shot is made or a participant is eliminated, the ball goes to the next person in line who takes a shot from the free throw line in his/her attempt to get the person in front of him/her out. The game continues until the winner is declared when one person remains after everyone else has been bumped out.

Discussion Topics

1. How did you feel when the cheating started?
2. Did you change the way you played once the cheating started?
3. If you were angry or frustrated, did you control it? How?
4. Is there ever a time in your life when you feel the need to get even? If so, what do you do and why do you do it?
5. What are the results of cheating or of getting even?
6. Instead of cheating or getting even when angry or frustrated, what could you do differently?
7. Did anyone recognize that cheating was going on? If so, was there any attempt made to change the situation?

KNOCK OUT

This is a quick game that is competitive and fun. Skill plays a role in this game and anyone who is less skilled may be frustrated. With only one winner left at the end, it's every person for him/herself. If someone gets frustrated or doesn't feel good about losing, make sure that they learn something about controlling their anger when they get knocked out of the game.

Objective

For people to display good sportsmanship towards others when involved in a physically aggressive game and to accept losing when eliminated in a competitive game. For people to practice using appropriate anger control skills when becoming frustrated, agitated or angry.

Who

People who have trouble losing.
People who have trouble controlling their anger in competitive situations.

Group Size

6 or more

Materials

- ➔ Four boundary markers (i.e. orange cones)
- ➔ One soccer ball for each participant

Description

Mark off a square, using the boundary markers, that is large enough for everyone to be in, with a couple of feet of space between each person. Start the game by giving each participant a ball which is his/hers to guard from all the others. The object of the game is to keep your ball in the boundary area while attempting to kick everybody else's ball out. Just as in soccer, no hands are allowed.

If your ball is kicked out, you are eliminated from the game. Once your ball is kicked out, you may not reenter the game until the next round is started. The winner is the last person to stay in without getting his/her ball kicked out. This game may go quickly so you may wish to play many rounds.

Discussion Topics

1. Was this a fun activity for you? Why or why not?
2. Do you feel that anyone was overly aggressive during the game? If so, how was it handled?
3. When in a game, is winning the most important thing? Why? Is this good or bad?
4. Are there times in your life when you or someone close to you becomes physically aggressive? Do you feel this behavior is appropriate? Why or why not?

Variations

➲ This game also works well with basketballs. Instead of kicking the basketballs participants dribble the basketballs in the area and attempt to hit the other balls out while they each are guarding their own ball closely.

➲ Play in teams with each team attempting to knock out everyone on the other team.

CREATIVE COMPETITION

It is not hard to find hostility at a sporting event these days. Parents of young children get angry at the referees, high school kids yell at the opponents' fans and people have even been killed in fights at professional sporting events. And those are the fans. The emotions of the people who are actually in the game may get even hotter.

Sports are a good place for people to practice anger control because their anger can be triggered easily when they are focused on beating the other team and winning the game. Group members should work on their sportsmanship in this activity.

Objective

For people to show good sportsmanship towards teammates and towards an opponent in a competitive situation. For people to practice using appropriate anger control skills when they are frustrated, agitated or angry.

Who

People who get angry about losing.
People who have trouble controlling their anger in competitive situations.

Group Size

Varies

Materials

➲ Varies

Description

Engage the group in any competitive game or sport. Make the focus of the game the use of good sportsmanship and appropriate anger control. You can use some of the activities listed below or one of the activities in the rest of this section.
➲ Soccer
➲ Basketball

- Flag Football
- Hockey
- Capture the Flag
- Softball
- Card games

Discussion Topics

1. What type of sportsmanship was displayed during the game and how was it displayed?
2. Was this game fun for you? Why or why not?
3. Did anyone feel frustrated or angry, for any reason, during this game? If so, why and how was it handled?
4. Do you feel competition is good or bad? Why?

TEAM CROQUET

When you have to depend on your teammates to help win a game, there is always a bigger chance of getting angry. There are simply more people to make mistakes. If you are very good at the game, it can be really hard not to get mad at teammates who are not as good. If you are not a good player, this can be really frustrating, too, because, even when you do your best, it may not be good enough. This activity lets the members of the group work on their interactions with teammates and a competing team.

Objective

For people to show good sportsmanship towards teammates and towards an opponent in a competitive situation. For people to practice using appropriate anger control skills when becoming frustrated, agitated or angry in a competitive activity.

Who

People who get frustrated by teammates with different levels of skill.

Group Size

4 to 6 participants

Materials

➲ Croquet set

Description

Set up the croquet game as you would for a normal game and allow participants to choose the color of mallet and ball. Once the colors are chosen, begin the game by dividing the group into two teams, so that every other color is on one team and every other color is on a second team. The idea is to help your team while attempting to knock the other team out. The first team to get all their team members through the course is the winner.

Discussion Topics

1. Were you concentrating more on helping your own teammates, on knocking the other team out or on your own play? Why?
2. Would you rather play as an individual or did you like playing as a team? Why?
3. What type of sportsmanship did you see displayed during the game?
4. How do you feel about yourself after winning or losing the game?
5. Did anyone feel frustrated or angry for any reason during the game? If so, why and how did you handle it?

GROUP FOOSBALL

Foosball is a competitive game that you can find at many recreation centers. This activity will let the group practice the game but, more importantly, it will give them a chance to practice controlling their anger when something goes wrong.

Objective

For people to show good sportsmanship towards teammates and towards an opponent in a competitive situation. For people to practice using appropriate anger control skills when becoming frustrated, agitated or angry in a competitive activity.

Who

People who have difficulty controlling their anger in competitive, team situations.

Group Size

4 to 8 participants

Materials

➲ Foosball table
➲ Foosballs

Description

Play foosball by regular foosball rules, with a team of players on each side of the table. Divide the group into two teams and assign each team member to one or two foosball handles on his/her team's side (i.e. if there are four people on a team, each person controls one handle). Keep score and play until one of the two teams reaches ten points.

Discussion Topics

1. What type of sportsmanship was displayed during the game and how was it displayed?
2. Did the members of your team work with other team members or work independently? Was this a benefit to the team or did it hurt the team?
3. Was this game fun for you? Why or why not?
4. Did anyone feel frustrated or angry for any reason during the game? If so, why and how did you handle it?

Variations

➲ May be used with a large group if two teams play at a time while additional teams sit out or participate in a different game while waiting to play the winning team.

THE BOARD GAME CHALLENGE

Not every competitive game is physically active. These games can be every bit as intense and frustrating as physical games. With these activities the group gets a chance to practice its anger management in another kind of realistic situation.

Objective

For people to show good sportsmanship towards teammates and towards an opponent in a competitive situation. For people to practice using appropriate anger control skills when becoming frustrated, agitated or angry in a competitive activity.

Who

People who have difficulty controlling their anger in competitive situations.

Group Size

3 or more

Materials

- Play money
- A variety of board games that are played by taking turns
- Some suggestions are Operation™, Stay Alive™, Simon™, Jenga™.

Description

The idea of the game is to finish with the most money. Money is earned by accomplishing different tasks from different games. For example if you are using the game Operation, pass the game around. Give each person a turn to pick out a piece without getting buzzed to earn a set amount of money.

This type of competition may be done with many different games. Use your imagination and resources to give away money using different board games. Money creates a competitive environment that seems to bring out intense feelings. Also a prize may be offered for the one with the most money at the end to increase the incentive and make the games a bit more competitive.

Discussion Topics

1. If you lost, how did you feel?
2. Why did you want to win?
3. Do you ever get angry or disappointed when playing a game? If so, how do you handle it?
4. Do you feel competition is good or bad? Why?
5. Would you have had the same desire to win if money had not been a factor? Why or why not?

Variations

➲ Hold an auction at the end of the game so that the group members can spend the money they won.
➲ Give away money for acts of good sportsmanship. Take away money for acts of poor sportsmanship.

PUZZLE RACE

A race can be a tense situation when you really want to win. This race is almost guaranteed to cause stress and frustration. When people are involved in a race as members of a team, it is important for them to keep their cool so they can work together and do the task as quickly as possible.

Objective

For people to show good sportsmanship towards teammates and towards opponents in a competitive situation. For people use appropriate anger control skills when becoming frustrated, agitated or angry.

Who

People who have difficulty with their anger in competitive situations.

Group Size

4 or more

Materials

- Jigsaw puzzle (50 to 100 pieces) for each team

Description

Divide the group into teams of two to four members, giving each team a jigsaw puzzle with the same number of pieces. On the signal to begin, each team tries to be the first to completely assemble its puzzle. You may wish to provide a prize for the winning team to encourage competition.

Discussion Topics

1. Was there ever a point when you or anyone on your team became frustrated or angry? If so, how was it handled?
2. Do you feel that there was good sportsmanship displayed during the puzzle race? Why or why not?
3. Did the competition affect how you worked with your teammates? Would it have been easier for you to work alone?

FiTNESS

Getting your shoes on and getting out the door seems to be the hardest part about exercising. Getting youth motivated and getting them to recognize that physical exercise has the potential to make them feel better emotionally, as well as physically, is just as difficult. Exercise can be a positive outlet and can serve as a much needed energy boost.

Exercise needs to be fun to get kids who are out-of-shape interested. Presenting a wide variety of different physically active games allows all the members of the group to find an activity that they enjoy. In addition to offering games that are fun, offer a variety of activities that are realistic for people to follow through with once they are no longer with the group. The fun games combined with the FEELiNGS CHECK are useful in getting youth inspired to use exercise as a means of coping with their issues. You may find that using fitness as a coping mechanism doesn't interest everyone and that's okay. Sparking interest in new activities, encouraging participation in an exercise routine and encouraging the use of exercise as a coping mechanism are the ultimate goals when presenting fitness to youth as a part of their treatment.

FITNESS ACTIVITIES

WHY WORKOUT

There are many different ways to work out and many different reasons. Some people want to look better. Some people know it makes them feel better. Some people do it because the activities are fun. Understanding why you choose to work out is important. Once group members realize that exercise can effect them in a positive way, mentally as well as physically, they may be more apt to exercise regularly as a way to improve their lives.

Objective

For people to explore and discuss why getting physical exercise may change how they feel emotionally as well as physically.

Who

People who are not sure why they should exercise.

Group Size

1 or more

Materials

- ➲ Paper
- ➲ Pens, pencils

Description

Provide each person with paper and a pen or pencil. Instruct the participants to write down all of the things that they have been involved in that they consider to be physical exercise on the left hand side of the paper. Once each person has come up with a list, ask them to write down the reasons that they were involved in each activity and how they felt after participating in the activity on the right hand side of the page.

Discussion Topics

1. Do you still participate in most of these activities? Why or why not?
2. Were most of the reasons that you participated in the activities positive or negative?
3. Did you list any activities that affected you emotionally as well as physically? What activity was it and how did it affect you?
4. If you wish to improve your physical activity list, how will you become more involved in physical activities?

FEELiNGS cHECK

Exercise can be a great form of stress release, anger release, and a great "pick me up" when we are down. Helping people to recognize the role that physical exercise can have in their lives is very important, especially for those who need to learn new ways of coping with the difficult things they face in their lives. Exercise is not the answer for everyone but it can certainly be a powerful tool for some people to incorporate into their lives.

Objective

For people to determine if engaging in a fitness activity has an effect on how they feel emotionally. To encourage people to engage in exercise to improve their own mental and physical health.

Who

People who could benefit from using exercise as a means to make them feel better emotionally as well as physically.

Group Size

1 or more

Materials

- ⊃ 3x5 cards
- ⊃ Pens or pencils

Description

Before a physical activity or game, ask each group member to write their name, how they feel emotionally and how they feel physically on a 3x5 card. Encourage the use of feeling words (i.e. happy, depressed, exhausted, etc.), discourage the use of words such as "fine" or "okay". If the group members have trouble finding descriptive words, you might use number scales from 1 to 10 for how they are feeling. Collect all of the cards once everyone has finished writing on them.

After this "feelings check," engage the group in an activity that requires some physical effort. The following pages contain some activity suggestions or you can use one of the activities in this list:

- Soccer
- Flag football
- Aerobics
- An obstacle course
- Basketball
- Fitness stations: If your facility has a weight center use it, if not be creative (i.e. jump rope, sit ups, jogging, push ups, etc.).

After the activity, gather the group back together and pass out the "feeling check" cards. Ask the group to look at how they felt before the activity and to notice if they feel different now that they have been physically active.

Discussion Topics

1. Do you feel any different after exercising than you did before exercising?
2. In what ways do you feel you have changed, physically or emotionally?
3. How can exercising regularly benefit you emotionally?
4. How can you begin an exercise routine if you do not already exercise on a regular basis?

Variations

- "Feelings check" may be verbal instead of written.

LiGHTNiNG

This is a high-energy, fun basketball game that can help members of the group see if exercise makes them feel better. Do it as part of the FEELiNGS CHECK activity or by itself for a fun fitness game.

Objective

For people to determine if engaging in a fitness activity has an effect on how they feel emotionally. To encourage people to engage in exercise to improve their own mental and physical health.

Who

People who could benefit from exercise.

Group Size

4 or more

Materials

➲ Two basketballs
➲ Basketball hoop

Description

Divide the group into two teams and line them up in separate single file lines at half court, facing the basketball hoop. The first person in each line has a basketball and, on the "go" signal, they both dribble their basketball to the end line (under the basket), back to the center line and then to the free throw line, where they each take a shot at the basket. After the first shot is taken they both keep shooting the ball from anywhere on the court until they each make a basket.

After a person makes a basket, s/he runs the ball to the next person in line, who continues the game. Each time a player returns to the line, s/he yells the number of shots his/her team has made and goes to the end of the line. The winning team is the first team to make twenty baskets.

Discussion Topics

1. Did you like this game? Why or why not?
2. Doing the FEELINGS CHECK, do you feel any different after exercising than you did before exercising?
3. In what ways do you feel you have changed, physically or emotionally?
4. How can exercising regularly benefit you emotionally?
5. Will you add this game to your regular set of exercises?

PiN SOCCER

This is a high-energy, fun (and slightly different) soccer game that the group can play to see if exercise makes them feel better. Even if the group is not that good at soccer, it can still be fun. Do it as part of the FEELiNGS CHECK activity or by itself for a fun fitness game.

Objective

For people to determine if engaging in a fitness activity has an effect on how they feel emotionally. To encourage people to engage in exercise to improve their own mental and physical health.

Who

People who could benefit from exercise.

Group Size

4 or more

Materials

- ➲ Bowling pin or pop bottle (2 liter size, filled 1/3 full with water, with the lid on) for each participant
- ➲ An assortment of balls

Description

Each participant is given a pin to place anywhere in the gymnasium or play area. Scatter the various balls around the play area. On the signal to begin play, each person attempts to guard his/her own pin, while at the same time attempting to knock over any of the other pins that others are guarding by using the balls and kicking them towards the pins. No hands are allowed during the game (as in regular soccer). Once a pin is knocked down, the owner of the pin is eliminated until the next round. The object of the game is to be the last person with a pin standing at the end of the game.

Discussion Topics

1. Did you like this game? Why or why not?
2. Doing the FEELINGS CHECK, do you feel any different after exercising than you did before exercising?
3. In what ways do you feel you have changed, physically or emotionally?
4. How can exercising regularly benefit you emotionally?
5. Will you add this game to your regular set of exercises?

Variations

➲ If there are more participants than there are bowling pins, then have those without a pin form a line at the edge of the play area. Once someone's pin is knocked down, they go to the end of the line and the first person in line takes his/her place and sets up the pin that was knocked over. Continue rotating in this manner until time runs out or the group tires out.

➲ Play in teams instead of individually. Divide the group into two teams and give each team the same number of pins. Each team places its pins on one side of the play area and must guard all of the pins while attempting to knock over the pins belonging to the other team. You may wish to make the rule that each team has to stay on its own side of the play area.

FOLLOW ME

This is a high-energy follow-the-leader game that the group can play to see if exercise makes them feel better. Do it as part of the FEELINGS CHECK activity or by itself for a fun fitness game.

Objective

For people to determine if engaging in a fitness activity has an effect on how they feel emotionally. To encourage people to engage in exercise to improve their own mental and physical health.

Who

People who could benefit from exercise.

Group Size

1 or more

Materials

➲ Varies

Description

Prior to the activity create a list of many exercises that can be done at your facility (some suggestions follow). Lead the group at a quick pace through the various exercises, going from one thing to the next with very little rest in between.

Exercise Suggestions:
➲ Jumping jacks
➲ Push ups
➲ Sit ups
➲ Shooting baskets
➲ Jumping rope

- Jogging
- Skipping
- Hopping on one foot
- Kicking a soccer ball back and forth

Discussion Topics

1. Did you like this game? Why or why not?
2. Doing the FEELiNGS CHECK, do you feel any different after exercising than you did before exercising?
3. In what ways do you feel you have changed, physically or emotionally?
4. How can exercising regularly benefit you emotionally?

Variations

- Let each person take a turn leading the exercises.

FLYING SAUCER

This is a high-energy, Frisbee™ Football game that the group can play to see if exercise makes them feel better. The more fun you are having, the easier getting exercise seems. This one is fun. Do it as part of the FEELINGS CHECK activity or by itself for a fun fitness game.

Objective

For people to determine if engaging in a fitness activity has an effect on how they feel emotionally. To encourage people to engage in exercise to improve their own mental and physical health.

Who

People who could benefit from exercise.

Group Size

6 or more

Materials

➲ Frisbee™
➲ Eight boundary makers

Description

Using the boundary markers, mark off a playing field that has a large open area with two end zone areas at each end like a football field. The size of the field will depend on the amount of space available and the size and ability of the group.

Divide the group into two teams, with the instructions to line up on their end line, facing the other team. One team starts with the Frisbee™ and throws it to the other team before running down the field. Once the receiving team gets the Frisbee™, they also run down the field and attempt to score a point. To score a point, the Frisbee™ must be thrown into the goal area and caught by one of the teammates of the person who threw it.

During the game, if the Frisbee™ ever hits the ground, it goes to the other team at that spot. Whoever has the Frisbee™ may only take three steps before throwing it to a teammate. If it isn't caught, it automatically goes to the other team. If it is caught, three steps may be taken before making a throw. Once a point is scored, the two teams line on their end lines. The team that scored throws to the other team and the game continues.

Discussion Topics

1. Did you like this game? Why or why not?
2. Doing the FEELINGS CHECK, do you feel any different after exercising than you did before exercising?
3. In what ways do you feel you have changed, physically or emotionally?
4. How can exercising regularly benefit you emotionally?
5. Will you add this game to your regular set of exercises?

TURBO BASKETBALL

This is a high-energy, fun basketball game that the group can play to see if exercise makes them feel better. If they thought basketball tired them out, wait until they try this game. Do it as part of the FEELINGS CHECK activity or by itself for a fun fitness game.

Objective

For people to determine if engaging in a fitness activity has an effect on how they feel emotionally. To encourage people to engage in exercise to improve their own mental and physical health.

Who

People who could benefit from exercise.

Group Size

4 to 12 participants (an even number is best)

Materials

⊃ Basketball
⊃ Basketball hoop

Description

Divide the group into two teams and pair each person up with a member of the other team. Play basketball by regular rules. However if your partner scores a basket you must go to the side line and do a set of exercises (2 push ups, 5 sit ups and 10 jumping jacks), before returning to the game. This is a good way to give the group exercise and allow them to have fun at the same time.

Discussion Topics

1. Did you like this game? Why or why not?
2. Is the game better when you have to do the exercises?
3. Doing the FEELiNGS cHECK, do you feel any different after exercising than you did before exercising?
4. In what ways do you feel you have changed, physically or emotionally?
5. How can exercising regularly benefit you emotionally?
6. Will you add this game to your regular set of exercises?

Variations

⮑ A different set of exercises may be done to better fit the needs of the group.
⮑ Soccer or any other sport that has two teams and a means of scoring may be used instead of basketball.
⮑ Whenever a point is scored, everyone on the other team must do a set of exercises.

RABBIT HUNT

This is a high-energy, capture and dodge ball game that the group can play to see if exercise makes them feel better. This one is more for younger people and it's a little easier physically than some of the other games in this section. Do it as part of the FEELINGS CHECK activity or by itself for a fun fitness game.

Objective

For people to determine if engaging in a fitness activity has an effect on how they feel emotionally. To encourage people to engage in exercise to improve their own mental and physical health.

Who

People who could benefit from exercise.

Group Size

8 or more

Materials

- ➲ Four boundary markers
- ➲ Two hula hoops or jump ropes
- ➲ Two soft rubber balls

Description

If you are in a gymnasium, use the walls as the boundaries for the game. If you are outside, set up two of the boundary markers at each end to form end lines. At the center of the playing field (on each side) place the two hula hoops or jump ropes laid out in a circle.

Select two participants to be the "hunters." Instruct them to each stand in one of the circles. Give each of the hunters a ball while the rest of the group lines up on one of the end lines. As soon as one of the hunters says "one, two, three, rabbit hunt," everyone on the end line attempts to run to the other line without being tagged by one of the balls that the hunters throw at them.

The hunters may only throw the ball when they are standing inside their circles and must retrieve it before throwing it again. Anyone who is hit with the ball must sit down in that spot. Those who have been tagged with the ball and are sitting down, may try to tag other runners by touching them as they run by. If someone is tagged by someone sitting s/he must also sit down. The last two to be standing are the hunters for the next game.

Discussion Topics

1. Did you like this game? Why or why not?
2. Doing the FEELINGS CHECK, do you feel any different after exercising than you did before exercising?
3. In what ways do you feel you have changed, physically or emotionally?
4. How can exercising regularly benefit you emotionally?
5. Will you add this game to your regular set of exercises?

DYNAMITE DISK GOLF

This is a fun, Frisbee™ Golf game that the group can play to see if exercise makes them feel better. It's for people who want some exercise, but not a seriously strenuous activity. Do it as part of the FEELINGS CHECK activity or by itself for a fun fitness game.

Objective

For people to determine if engaging in a fitness activity has an effect on how they feel emotionally. To encourage people to engage in exercise to improve their own mental and physical health.

Who

People who could benefit from exercise.

Group Size

2 or more

Materials

➲ One Frisbee™ per person (a variety of colors is best)

Description

Gather the group together outside at a designated point and pass out the Frisbees™. Select a spot that the group members will be attempting to hit with their Frisbees™ (i.e. tree, light post, garbage can, bench, etc.). Each person takes a turn to throw his/her Frisbee™ towards the target in an attempt to hit it with the Frisbee™.

Once everyone has taken their first turn, everyone takes their second turn from the spot where their own Frisbee™ landed. Each person takes as many turns as needed to successfully hit the target. Once everyone hits the first target, start from that point and select another target to throw towards. Continue the game until time runs out or you play eighteen "holes".

Discussion Topics

1. Did you like this game? Why or why not?
2. Doing the FEELINGS CHECK, do you feel any different after exercising than you did before exercising?
3. In what ways do you feel you have changed, physically or emotionally?
4. How can exercising regularly benefit you emotionally?
5. Will you add this game to your regular set of exercises?

SPiDER BALL

This is a high-energy, fun game that the group can play to see if exercise makes them feel better. One of the best parts is that, even if you are out of the game, there are still ways to get back in. Do it as part of the FEELiNGS CHECK activity or by itself for a fun fitness game.

Objective

For people to determine if engaging in a fitness activity has an effect on how they feel emotionally. To encourage people to engage in exercise to improve their own mental and physical health.

Who

People who could benefit from exercise.

Group Size

6 or more

Materials

➲ soft rubber ball

Description

One person is selected to start with the ball; s/he attempts to tag others by throwing the ball. Anyone who does not have the ball is free to run anywhere in the play area but the person with the ball may only take three steps before throwing it. Once a player is hit by the ball, s/he must sit down in that spot. When the ball is loose, anyone may grab it in an attempt to use it to get others out.

Anyone who is sitting may rejoin the game at any time by grabbing the ball as it rolls by, throwing it from a sitting position and hitting someone who is standing. The winner is the last person standing, who then begins the next game as the person with the ball.

Discussion Topics

1. Did you like this game? Why or why not?
2. Doing the FEELINGS CHECK, do you feel any different after exercising than you did before exercising?
3. In what ways do you feel you have changed, physically or emotionally?
4. How can exercising regularly benefit you emotionally?
5. Will you add this game to your regular set of exercises?

PiCK A PACKET

Many magazines have exercises and stretches that can be done individually. Since group members may not have access to a gym or a workout room, having a set of exercises that they can do other places will make it easier for them to exercise regularly. If you can, do your workout as part of the FEELiNGS CHECK activity to see if it meets the group's needs.

Objective

For each individual to create an exercise routine that can be followed once the individual is no longer with the group.

Who

People who are planning an exercise program for themselves.

Group Size

1 or more

Materials

- ➲ A variety of fitness magazines and books that can be copied
- ➲ Paper
- ➲ Pens, pencils
- ➲ Scissors
- ➲ Access to a copy machine

Description

Each person prepares a packet of exercises that they can do by themselves when they are no longer with the group. Provide a stack of magazines and books that contain a variety of exercises. Allow time for people to select exercises that they want to put into their packet and to mark pages so that a copy can be made of the exercises. If possible, provide group time for the people to do the workout that they have created prior to doing it at home. This will help them get started and see if they really like the workout they selected.

Discussion Topics

1. Why did you pick the exercises you chose?
2. Do you think it will provide a balanced set of exercises that you will be able to do regularly?

If you have a chance to do the exercise set:
1. Did you like your set of exercises?
2. Is there anything that you want to change?

TURBO GAMES

Sometimes one game is just not enough. This activity lets the group try a lot of games one after the other to see if exercise makes them feel better. Do it as part of the FEELINGS CHECK activity or by itself for a fun fitness game.

Objective

For people to determine if engaging in a fitness activity has an effect on how they feel emotionally. To encourage people to engage in exercise to improve their own mental and physical health.

Who

People who could benefit from exercise.

Group Size

4 or more

Materials

➲ Varies

Description

Create a list of a variety of active games that are fast paced and fun (i.e. LIGHTNING, RABBIT HUNT, SPIDER BALL, any sort of tag game, etc.). Lead the group in playing each game for a short period of time before quickly moving on to the next game. This keeps kids interested and allows them to get a great amount of exercise at the same time.

Discussion Topics

1. Did you like these games? Why or why not?
2. Did you like changing games lots of times?
3. Doing the FEELINGS CHECK, do you feel any different after exercising than you did before exercising?
4. In what ways do you feel you have changed, physically or emotionally?
5. How can exercising regularly benefit you emotionally?

ALPHABETICAL LIST OF GAMES

THE WRECKING YARD